TAXCafe™

Taxcafe.co.uk Tax Guides

The World's Best Tax Havens

How to Cut Your Taxes to Zero and Safeguard Your Financial Freedom

By Lee Hadnum LLB ACA CTA

Important Legal Notices:

TAXCafe
TAX GUIDE – "The World's Best Tax Havens"

Published by:
Taxcafe UK Limited
214 High St
Kirkcaldy KY1 1JT
United Kingdom
Tel: (01592) 560081

First edition   February 2006

ISBN 1 904608 29 9

Trademarks
The logo "TAXCafe " is a trademark of Taxcafe UK Limited. All other logos, trademarks, names and logos in this Tax Guide may be trademarks of their respective owners.

Disclaimer
Before reading or relying on the content of this Tax Guide, please read carefully the disclaimer on the last page which applies. If you have queries then please contact the publisher at team@taxcafe.co.uk.

Other Taxcafe.co.uk guides by the same author

Using a Company to Save Tax

How to Avoid Tax on Your Stock Market Profits

Non-Resident & Offshore Tax Planning

Dedication

This book is dedicated to my wife, Sharon Hadnum, who has been my supporting foundation for many years.

About the Author

Lee Hadnum is a key member of the Taxcafe.co.uk team. Apart from authoring a number of our tax guides, he also provides personalised tax guidance through our popular Question & Answer Service, a role he carries out with a great deal of enthusiasm and professionalism.

Lee is a rarity among tax advisers having both legal AND chartered accountancy qualifications. After qualifying as a prize winner in the Institute of Chartered Accountants entrance exams, he went on to become a Chartered Tax Adviser (CTA).

Having worked in Ernst & Young's tax department for a number of years, Lee decided to start his own tax consulting firm, specialising in capital gains tax, inheritance tax and offshore tax planning.

He also tutors at a number of accountancy colleges in the north-west of England.

Whenever he has spare time Lee enjoys DIY, walking and travelling.

Contents

Contents (contd)

Introduction

Offshore tax planning has become increasingly popular over the years as more and more wealthy individuals seek to escape the high taxes imposed in many of the wealthy developed countries.

Offshore tax planning has two key components:

- Understanding the tax rules in your current country of residence, and
- Understanding the tax regimes of other countries.

This book is concerned mainly with the second component: identifying countries that have low tax rates and offer you the opportunity to pay less tax.

We'll be looking at where you should go and live or buy property if you want to pay as little tax as possible. We'll also look at how offshore trusts, companies and other structures can be used.

Wealth Warning!

Always remember that your home country's tax laws will affect your ability to use tax havens.

Always seek professional advice before you act. International tax is a complex area and no book can cover all the angles.

What is a Tax Haven?

At the outset we need to explain what is meant by the phrase 'tax haven' and summarise the benefits they offer before identifying the countries and tax planning techniques in more detail.

A tax haven is simply a country that allows you to reduce the amount of tax you pay.

This is a tax haven at its most basic and, although pretty obvious, it's worth bearing in mind what their purpose is without getting bogged down in the details.

Let's state at the beginning that there is nothing wrong with using tax havens provided you are careful not to break any rules in your country of residence.

Many people use tax havens to hide their money from the tax authorities in their home countries. This is not only illegal, it's foolish because one day you probably will get caught and could end up with substantial fines or even a jail sentence.

However, if you have the legal right to use a tax haven you would be foolish not to take advantage of all the opportunities you can to maximise your wealth.

There are three main types of tax haven:

- Nil-tax havens
- Foreign source exempt havens
- Low-tax havens

Nil-tax Havens

These are simply countries that do not have any of the three main direct taxes:

- No income tax or corporation tax
- No capital gains tax, and
- No inheritance tax

Many of the nil tax havens you've probably heard of or read about in novels. You may even have holidayed in some of them. They include:

- The Cayman Islands
- St Kitts and Nevis
- Dubai
- Monaco
- The Bahamas
- Bermuda
- Vanuatu
- The Turks & Caicos Islands
- Anguilla

Although there are no taxes in these jurisdictions, the tax haven governments still need to generate some revenue to provide public services. They may therefore impose small fees for company incorporation documents or annual registration fees for companies. However, these charges are fixed and usually small.

In addition there may be import duties or even local sales taxes.

Foreign Source Exempt Havens

These countries do levy taxes and sometimes they can be pretty high. However, what makes them tax havens is the fact they only tax you on *locally derived income*.

In other words, if all your income is derived outside the tax haven you will not pay any tax. Good examples of foreign source exempt tax havens are:

- Panama
- Costa Rica
- Hong Kong
- Singapore

This type of tax haven exempts from tax any income earned from foreign sources, provided (and this is crucial) the foreign income source does not involve any local business activity.

For example, you couldn't set up a consultancy business that was run from Panama and claim that the income generated shouldn't be subject to tax there.

Some of the other tax havens don't even allow a company to conduct business internally if any tax advantages are to be claimed.

Jurisdictions such as Jersey, Guernsey, the Isle of Man and Gibraltar would require a company to decide at the time of incorporation whether it was allowed to do local business (and therefore taxed on its worldwide profits), or only foreign business and therefore free from taxation.

Low-tax Havens

The final group of tax havens are countries that do have a system of taxation and impose taxes on residents' worldwide income. You may be wondering why these are still classed as tax havens. There are two main reasons:

- Some countries may have special concessions that offer considerable tax advantages in *special situations* (such as for capital gains tax avoidance).
- Clever use of double tax treaties that countries enter into with each other may allow you to *lower* your tax bill.

The problem with the well-known nil-tax havens is most developed countries do not have treaties with them. When planning your tax affairs it may be more tax efficient to use a low-tax haven, combined with a double tax treaty, than simply rely on a nil-tax haven.

Example

Let's say you own shares in a company listed on the London or New York Stock Exchange. For commercial reasons (in other words, non-tax reasons) you want to set up a holding company to own the shares. You could use one of the traditional tax havens such as the Bahamas or the Cayman Islands. The problem with using these countries is that UK or US withholding tax will be deducted from dividends at rates of up to 25%.

However, if you use one of the recognised holding company jurisdictions, such as Belgium or Denmark, there will be very little or no tax deducted in the UK or US. Good examples of low-tax havens are:

- Cyprus
- The United Kingdom
- Barbados
- Switzerland
- Denmark
- Belgium
- The Netherlands
- Austria

Other Important Factors to Consider

When looking at tax havens, although the amount of tax they levy is obviously crucial, this is not the only important factor.

You wouldn't, for example, want to invest your cash in an offshore account in a politically unstable country, particularly if there is a risk that your assets could be expropriated.

Therefore tax planning is only one consideration. Other important factors include:

- **Privacy.** What level of disclosure is there. Will your financial affairs be kept private from prying eyes?

- **Ease of residence.** How easy is it to obtain permission to live in the tax haven?

- **Political stability.** Is there a risk your cash could end up in the government's coffers?

- **Communications.** How good is telephone and broadband internet access and how easy is it to travel to the country?

- **Lifestyle factors.** If you want to live there, how good is schooling, the climate, and how high is the cost of living?

It's therefore a question of what you want from your tax haven: are you only concerned with the tax position or are other factors equally important?

I mention some of these other factors elsewhere in the book, although obviously many of these are subjective and would therefore need to be addressed by you personally. We'll therefore mainly be focusing on the tax issues.

Chapter 1

How Tax Havens Can Help You

In this chapter we'll take a brief look at how tax havens can be used to cut your tax bill. The chapters that follow contain much more detailed information but I think it's worth explaining some of the tax planning techniques briefly before we look at some of the individual tax havens.

Most countries will tax you in one of three different ways, based on:

- **The source of your income or capital gains.** If your income is derived locally the local tax authorities will tax you on it.

- **Your country of residence.** If you are resident in a country, that country may have the right to tax you on your worldwide income or gains. The United Kingdom does this.

- **Your country of nationality.** This is rare, but is very important if it applies. Some countries such as the United States tax you if you are a national or citizen. Even if you leave the country you will still have to pay tax.

Most developed countries apply the first two rules, although the US applies all three in certain situations. It's easy to see how two countries could easily decide to tax the same income.

Example

Steve, a UK resident, has an offshore bank account in Spain. As a resident of the UK he will be liable to UK tax on his worldwide income, including his Spanish interest.

However as the interest has a Spanish source, Spain will also want to tax it. In this case the double tax treaty between the two countries would come to the rescue. Any Spanish tax paid would be allowed as a credit against Steve's UK tax liability.

What if Steve used a bank in a nil-tax haven such as the Bahamas or the Cayman Islands?

In this case there would be no overseas tax as these countries do not levy tax. However, there would still be UK taxes to pay because individuals who are UK resident and domiciled are subject to UK tax on their worldwide income.

This is crucial to understand because it dispels the myth that tax havens can be used to automatically escape taxes. Unless you are careful how you use them you will not enjoy any tax savings.

Some books hint at keeping your income private and therefore hint at tax evasion. In many countries this is the fastest way to land in jail (or at the very least end up paying substantial penalties) and I would never advise this.

You should always disclose as much information as the tax authorities in your home country require.

Every country has different disclosure requirements. For example, the US requires separate disclosure of foreign bank accounts of which you are a signatory. Other countries such as the UK do not.

It's the secrecy that European and North American tax departments don't like and this has led to growth in tax information agreements between countries and, for example, the advent of the EU Savings Tax Directive.

In terms of this agreement members of the EU (and various overseas dependencies) will automatically share information with each other about customers who earn savings income in one country but live in another.

Provided you stick to these simple rules you should be able to sleep peacefully at night. And that's far more important than escaping tax!

Tax havens are useful in lots of different ways, including:

Emigration

If you fancy living abroad, one option is to live in a tax haven. Fortunately many tax havens have extremely high living standards and are beautiful places to stay. If you choose the country wisely, you may be able to completely avoid income tax and other taxes.

Emigrating to one of the nil-tax havens such as the Bahamas, St Kitts and Nevis, the Cayman Islands or the British Virgin Islands would be ideal for this purpose. US citizens cannot do this, however, because they are subject to US tax wherever they live (although there are limited tax exemptions for US citizens living abroad that can exempt the first $80,000 of earned income).

Another option may be to establish yourself in one of the foreign source exempt havens and put your money in an offshore bank account. In this way you will also not pay one penny in tax.

Finally, you could go and live in a low-tax haven if it offers concessions that suit your particular circumstances. For example, you could go and live in South Africa or New Zealand if you have a big property investment portfolio and want to escape capital gains tax.

Diverting Profits

Tax havens are often used to divert profits from a country with high tax rates to a country with low tax rates. They're also used to divert interest, royalties and management charges.

Unfortunately this is not very easy to do in practice – the country where the income is sourced is likely to have rules that prevent you from doing this. However, it is possible in certain circumstances.

Example

Patrick owns a company called Compco that manufactures and sells computers. His company is located in a country with a corporation tax of 30%. Patrick decides to become non-resident and live in a tax haven, while still doing work for the company.

The advantage is that there will be no income tax to pay in the tax haven. Furthermore, provided the cost of his services is set at a reasonable commercial rate, Compco will be allowed a tax deduction for the full amount paid to Patrick. This means there will be no corporation tax on the money paid to Patrick.

Diverting income from a high-tax country to a low-tax country is one of the key benefits of using offshore tax havens.

Double Tax Treaty (DTT) Manipulation

As mentioned earlier, low-tax havens are often used to take advantage of double tax treaties. Using double tax treaties to avoid taxes can result in big savings and this makes some of the low tax destinations that have lots of double tax treaties very popular.

Example

Pedro conducts business in the United States but through an offshore company located in Cyprus.

Provided Pedro does not actually have a fixed place of business in the United States (the treaty defines this as having a 'permanent establishment' in the US – more on this later in the book!) the income from the business will pass to that company with little or no US tax being paid because of the tax treaty between the two countries.

If income is paid to a person or company in a jurisdiction with no tax treaty with the US, the profits will be subject to US tax, at a rate as high as 35%.

Now that the money is sitting in the Cyprus company, it could be extracted free of Cypriot taxes to a non-resident.

This example illustrates how complex offshore tax planning with tax havens can be. Everyone's situation is different, hence the need for professional advice.

Capital Gains Tax (CGT) Planning

In recent years many individuals have moved abroad to escape capital gains tax. Most are property investors who have made huge profits during the global real estate boom of recent years.

If they sold their properties without moving they'd see a large chunk of their profits going to the taxman in their country of residence or the country where the property is located.

Avoiding a big tax bill is particularly important where properties have been heavily remortgaged to enable the investor to withdraw the equity (paper profits).

Investors with large debts over some properties may actually end up with insufficient cash to cover their capital gains tax bills. Therefore they look for any opportunity, including moving overseas, to escape paying tax.

Tax havens are also used to escape CGT by entrepreneurs who've had enough of the rat race and want to sell their companies.

Using offshore company arrangements or emigrating to countries that don't charge CGT on overseas disposals can drastically reduce the tax liability.

Example

Tony, a UK resident, has a big property portfolio with profits in excess of £1 million.

He wants to sell the properties and minimize the tax payable by moving offshore.

The UK doesn't usually impose capital gains tax on non-residents (unless they're conducting a trade from the UK) and Tony therefore decides to move to the Bahamas, sell his property portfolio and avoid paying UK capital gains tax.

The downside to this is that he would need to stay overseas for five complete UK tax years to avoid the gains being taxed if he returns.

Five years is too long for many people. It used to be possible to get around this by emigrating to a country with a suitable tax treaty with the UK (Greece was one such country). Unfortunately the UK closed this loophole in the 2004 Pre Budget Report and UK emigrants are therefore usually tied in to a five year absence. (Having said that, they could still spend up to three months per tax year in the UK without bringing the gain back within the scope of UK taxes.)

Inheritance Tax (IHT) Planning

If there's one tax people resent above all others it's inheritance tax. Paying 40% tax on your **assets** is much worse than paying 40% tax on your **profits**. Furthermore, your assets will, for the most part, have been built up out of after-tax income – meaning that they are effectively taxed twice.

The good news is there are ways that tax havens can help you reduce your inheritance tax bill. By transferring some of your wealth into an offshore trust or company you can escape the tax in certain circumstances because the trust/company becomes the new owner of the assets. Your estate will then have fewer assets to tax.

Many countries don't subject offshore trusts and companies to IHT and, if they do, it's usually an amended form of tax. Hence the correct use of offshore entities can maximize your wealth and minimize your taxes.

Once again it's important to stress that offshore tax planning is a complicated area and you should always obtain detailed professional advice from a qualified tax adviser in your country of residence.

In particular, there will probably be anti-avoidance rules (most high-tax countries have them) that may apply and careful 'navigation' in these circumstances is essential.

Asset Protection

Tax havens aren't just used by people who want to pay less tax. They're also very important for the purposes of *asset protection*.

You'll notice that the subtitle of this book says 'Safeguard Your Financial Freedom'.

We're not referring to saving tax here but to the importance of protecting your wealth from anyone else who may try to get their hands on it.

In recent years the UK has gone much the same way as the US and become litigation crazy.

Doctors and other professionals feel extremely vulnerable but anyone could fall victim to a frivolous lawsuit.

Others who may try to target you include ex-employees, spouses or business partners, fraudsters and other crooks, disgruntled family members or clients, ambulance-chasing lawyers and virtually anyone who knows you have money and thinks you are easy prey.

The idea of asset protection is to make your assets extremely difficult to trace and, if they are traced, extremely difficult to get hold of.

For example, many tax havens have strict banking secrecy laws and as long as you are not involved in any criminal activity or money laundering your details will not be made available to third parties.

There are, of course, things you can do in your home country to protect your wealth, for example setting up a limited company or limited liability partnership.

However, many argue that nothing quite beats the privacy of setting up an offshore structure, especially if you choose a tax haven with strong privacy laws. Your creditors first have to find your offshore company, trust or bank account before they can get their hands on your money!

It's important to bear this point in mind as you read the book. You may not be able to use a tax haven to legally avoid tax... but you may be able to use one to protect your money from everyone else.

Chapter 2

The World's Best Tax Havens

Now that we've looked at some of the ways tax havens are used it's time to take a look at the individual countries and find out what they offer.

In the sections that follow we'll be looking at the following countries:

- Andorra
- Anguilla
- The Bahamas
- Barbados
- Belize
- Bermuda
- The British Virgin Islands (BVI)
- The Cayman Islands
- The Cook Islands
- Costa Rica
- Cyprus
- Dubai
- Eastern Europe
- Gibraltar
- Guernsey/Jersey
- Ireland
- Isle of Man
- Liechtenstein
- Malta
- Monaco
- Panama
- St Kitts and Nevis
- Switzerland
- Turks and Caicos Islands (TCI)

We'll also be exploring a few of the 'alternative' tax havens.

ANDORRA

If you're wealthy and want to escape government red tape and high taxes, Andorra could be the place to go.

It's a small country (less than 35 miles long) and most people live along a single road linking France and Spain. Some residents complain that this can make living there a little claustrophobic!

Andorra has no income tax, capital gains tax, gift tax, inheritance tax or capital transfer tax. Employees pay national insurance contributions and there are some limited municipal taxes on property.

So for all intents and purposes, Andorra can be described as a nil-tax haven.

Many residents have properties in France and Spain, which they escape to at the weekend. As a result the roads are often congested at these times. However, lots of the upper valleys are quiet and very beautiful and a walkers' and skiers' paradise.

Andorra seems to avoid much of the barmy EU regulation and red tape by hiding away in the mountains. The climate is excellent with lots of winter (and summer) sunshine and is surprisingly dry. People with chest complaints go there for health reasons. There is a lot of winter snow, although this does tend to be limited to the upper mountains.

The nearest international airports are Toulouse and Barcelona, 3½ hours and 3 hours away by road respectively.

From a tax perspective, Andorra is certainly attractive, in particular for Europeans not wanting to move too far from home.

In addition as a place to squirrel away your savings, Andorra is hard to beat. There are no exchange controls and the banks also offer numbered accounts (accounts that have no name and just a number).

The country does, however, have some strict anti-money-laundering legislation aimed at criminals, although this excludes tax avoidance, which is not a crime in Andorra.

Most expatriates who go to Andorra for tax reasons (also known as 'passive' residents) live in the La Massna or Ordino parishes, where property prices are higher than elsewhere although still quite reasonable.

Property prices have risen by about 10% per year over the last 10 years (in sterling terms). Despite this steady growth, property in Andorra is still far more reasonably priced than in other European tax havens such as Monaco.

A modern three-bedroom apartment costs from £250,000 and will usually include basement parking (essential in winter) and be finished to a high standard. A good view or garden would add considerably to the price.

Individual houses are rare and cost from £800,000 to £1 million. Large modern properties with good fittings and views command exceptional prices.

Cheaper property is available in other parts of the country, notably in the town centres and ski areas (these properties are unlikely to suit the sort of person coming to Andorra to escape tax – owning a ski apartment could be detrimental to your residence application).

There is a 2.5% tax on property transfers, although this is likely to go up with the Government proposing a rate of 4%.

One of the biggest drawbacks to using Andorra as a tax haven is obtaining residence there. They have tight restrictions on who they let in. Tourist visas are relatively simple to obtain but for a longer-term stay it's necessary to have either a work permit or a Passive Residence Permit (PRP).

Work permits are notoriously difficult to get. They are usually only issued to EU nationals and then only if there is no Andorran who is qualified to do the job.

Work permits are given only to individuals working for an Andorran person or company and are not given to self-employed foreigners.

In practice, if you want to live in Andorra permanently, especially if you plan to live off your investments, you will need to obtain a passive residence permit.

Obtaining passive residence is a bureaucratic process that requires some patience. If you're looking into this it's probably worth employing the services of an experienced agent who can guide you through the process.

Residence is initially granted for one year and renewed every three years after that. You will need to sign an undertaking to live in Andorra for at least six months per year and, although few checks are carried out, recent utility bills are examined at renewal time.

Among the list of requirements is that a couple deposit €30,000 with the Government. No interest is paid but the money is returned when you leave.

You must also be able to demonstrate an income of more than three times the average wage, currently a minimum income of €37,600 (for a couple).

In practice this means having that sum in the bank when residence permits are renewed (as a bank certificate is required).

You will also need to own or rent a house in Andorra and take out health insurance.

All in all, Andorra is one of the top European tax havens, particularly for UK residents not looking to move too far.

One point to bear in mind, however, is that there is a relatively small expat community. So if you only speak English the social scene may be somewhat limited.

Note that Andorra is ideally placed for individual residence, but less so for corporate residence as the country does not have any double tax treaties. For example, if you want to set up a holding company, there would be reduced opportunities to avoid withholding taxes.

ANGUILLA

Most people have never heard of Anguilla. It's a British overseas territory in the north-eastern Caribbean and is only 16 miles long.

If beaches are your thing, this place will be right up your street – it has over 30 of them. And as you'd expect it's pretty hot with an average temperature of 80 degrees and low rainfall.

To top it all Anguilla also has some of the most reasonably priced property in the Caribbean. Beautiful properties can be snapped up for a fraction of the price you would pay on one of the better-known Caribbean islands.

As for tax, Anguilla is about as good as it gets. It's one of the nil-tax havens which means there is no:

- Income tax
- Inheritance or other estate taxes
- Capital gains tax
- Gift tax, or
- Corporation tax

So if you're thinking about moving overseas and living off your investments, you could enjoy a totally tax-free lifestyle if you based yourself there.

Anguilla is also a popular location for trusts, in particular Asset Protection Trusts (APTs). This type of trust is often set up by wealthy doctors, lawyers and dentists who want to protect their assets from negligence claims or anyone else who wants to protect their assets from spurious lawsuits and the like.

Anguilla is one of the top jurisdictions for such trusts, mainly because of its strict privacy laws. The courts in Anguilla only allow very restricted claims against trusts if the claim relates to divorce, debts or overseas taxes.

Anguilla doesn't have any double tax treaties but it does have excellent banks and financial services. There are well over 100 banks there, including such prestigious names as Barclays and Bank of America.

The fact that it is a British dependency also adds comfort to some, as this reduces the likelihood of any civil unrest, given the protection promised by the British Government.

If you're moving to Anguilla from one of the more developed countries, such as the United Kingdom or the USA, one of the big attractions may also be the low crime. The island has one of the lowest crime rates in the world.

Although property prices are quite reasonable they have been shooting up in the last couple of years, as more and more people cotton on to the fact that the island has a high standard of living as well as being one of the best tax havens around.

You're looking at paying between $200,000 and $300,000 for a nice three- to four-bedroom property close to the beach. As a non-Anguillan, bear in mind you would also need to pay an additional 12.5% property transfer tax (this is one of the ways the government raises revenue without charging taxes on income).

Furthermore, there are restrictions on the *type* of property you can buy. In particular, beachfront homes cannot be bought by foreigners.

Obtaining residence in Anguilla is not easy and unlike other Caribbean jurisdictions there is no minimum number of days you have to spend there in order to be classed as a resident.

If you want to work on the island you need to obtain a work permit and, as with most Caribbean destinations, the authorities are reluctant to issue one if they think you'll be taking jobs away from locals (although if you're working in a specialised field a more relaxed attitude will be taken).

If you want to obtain permanent residence you'll need to buy a property and apply for a permanent residence certificate. This will allow easier exit and entry through Customs when you leave Anguilla but could also be shown to overseas tax authorities to back up your claim to being resident abroad.

Given the fact that Anguilla is becoming a popular tax haven, obtaining local tax advice is not difficult. You'll find some of the world's biggest law and accounting firms have offices on the island (although be prepared to pay at least $500-$750 per hour for tax-planning services).

If you're looking for an offshore company located in a tax-free jurisdiction Anguilla offers an International Business Company (IBC), which allows trading outside Anguilla free of Anguillan tax. Not a good choice as a holding company, however, as there are no double tax treaties, but a useful type of company if you're looking for local tax and asset protection.

Of more importance is that Anguilla also offers a limited liability company (LLC). Not all jurisdictions offer these. An LLC is basically a cross between a company and a partnership. It offers the limited liability protection of a company (because it's a separate legal entity) yet for tax purposes is treated like a partnership. This means the income is taxed in the hands of the members of the LLC according to their residence status. Losses would also 'pass through' to the members.

THE BAHAMAS

The Bahamas is made up of about 700 islands and 2,500 cays which are spread over 750 miles of the Atlantic Ocean. Only a few of these islands are actually inhabited.

The Bahamas is one of the top Caribbean tax havens and, like Anguilla, is a nil-tax haven. So there's no:

- Income tax
- Corporation tax
- Capital gains tax
- Inheritance tax

Lots of countries class themselves as having low taxation. However, the Bahamas truly is a zero-tax jurisdiction and it doesn't even levy any sales taxes. And this favourable state of affairs applies to everyone, including companies and trusts.

There are excellent travel links and the airport has half a dozen daily flights to Miami and other major destinations such as London and New York.

For US residents the Bahamas are particularly attractive because it's the closest tax haven to the United States. It can take as little as 45 minutes to fly from Florida to Nassau.

If you're thinking of moving to the Bahamas you can expect plenty of sun and an outdoor way of life. Activities such as tennis, basketball, scuba diving, golf, snorkelling, fishing and cricket are all popular.

Escaping crime is a key factor for many emigrants and while the Bahamas has relatively low crime, it can still be an issue. It's more of a problem in Nassau, especially with the high level of drug use amongst some locals.

The Sting in the Tail – Import Duties

Although the Bahamas has practically no taxation, the Government still needs to raise revenue from somewhere. It does this by charging company licence fees, stamp duty, property taxes and, worst of all, sky-high import duties.

Import duties average 40% so if you're planning on living in the Bahamas the main issue is likely to be the high cost of living.

As always it will depend on the lifestyle that you choose. If you expect to live in the same way as you did in the UK or US and eat similar foods etc, you will end up paying through the nose for imported products. If you adapt and eat local produce, it will cost you much less.

Having said that, there isn't much that is cheap in the Bahamas. For example, rents are pretty steep with a small ocean apartment costing in the region of $3,000 to $4,000 per month.

The Bahamas are one of the most popular of the Caribbean tax havens. The banking sector is huge and has acquired an excellent reputation as a location for offshore banking.

However, it's fair to say that its appeal has weakened slightly among US residents following the signing of a tax information and exchange agreement (IEA) with the American Government.

Nevertheless, the Bahamas still offers excellent confidentiality to residents of other countries.

The IEA allows the US Internal Revenue Service to obtain details of offshore accounts held by US residents and effectively overrules the strict banking secrecy usually in place in the Bahamas.

Note that many of the 'larger' tax havens have signed the IEA including the Cayman Islands, Bermuda and Jersey. If you're looking for a nil-tax haven that has not, try Anguilla which although covered by the UK-US mutual legal assistance treaty, expressly excludes tax offences.

To become resident in the Bahamas you would need to obtain a residence permit. This can be difficult unless you are sent to work there or are prepared to invest substantial sums of money.

Generally jobs are not open to foreigners, unless you have a particular skill that is not available locally.

With the advent of the internet, many people looking to emigrate also plan to work remotely. If you are 'telecommuting' you will not need a work permit, as your company is not trading in the Bahamas and your income comes from overseas.

If you do need a residence permit you'll need to apply to the Immigration Board. Unless you're a major international investor or are planning to purchase a property in the Bahamas for at least $500,000, issue of a residence permit is unlikely.

Property in the Bahamas tends to be more expensive than in other Caribbean countries (except for the Cayman Islands), and you could expect to pay roughly $1 million for a nice four-bedroom beachfront property.

Just as in Anguilla, if you're looking for a tax-free offshore company, a Bahamanian International Business Company (IBC) may be just what you're looking for. With traditionally good financial privacy, the Bahamas is a popular location for non-resident companies.

BARBADOS

Barbados is another popular offshore financial centre. If you want to live in a cosmopolitan environment with a tropical climate, low crime and don't mind paying high living costs this may just be the place for you.

Barbados is firmly in the 'low tax' or, more accurately, 'some tax' category. So you're likely to be stung for some taxes – but you can save on others that would normally be paid in other countries.

In particular, Barbadian residents don't pay any

- Capital gains tax, or
- Inheritance tax and gift tax.

However, the authorities do levy income tax and VAT (a form of sales tax). To a certain extent there is a trade off, as if you want to live in a well-developed country with a good telephone network, a relatively good road and transportation network and good schools you're going to have to pay some tax.

Having said that, income tax in Barbados is not low by any standards. The rate is 20% on income up to $24,200 and 37.5% on income above $24,200. Some people would therefore end up paying more income tax in Barbados than they would in the US or the UK. So you're probably wondering why would anyone bother moving to Barbados to escape tax?

Well aside from the fact that there is no capital gains tax or inheritance tax, if you're resident but *non-domiciled* in Barbados you'll only be taxed on overseas income that you actually bring into the country.

This means an emigrant can often completely avoid income tax by keeping income out of Barbados.

In terms of residence, the traditional definition applies with an individual becoming Barbadian resident for the whole year after spending more than 182 days there during a calendar year (which in Barbados is the same as the tax year).

Note that the top rate of income tax (37.5% in 2005) is to be reduced to 35% for 2006. However, it's still very high, particularly for an offshore centre and unless you use the non-domicile rules there are very few income tax savings to be had and it would then mainly be of benefit to individuals looking to avoid capital gains tax.

If you want to work there you will also have to pay social security contributions. These are pretty high and in the region of 10%.

Although these will be of less importance to immigrants looking to retire abroad, if you're thinking about setting up a business offshore and possibly employing staff, social security is an additional cost to take into account.

Barbados also has stamp duty and property transfer tax which is set at 5% (for residents) on the conveyance of land.

Unlike the nil-tax havens Barbados does have some double tax treaties, however these are pretty few and far between when compared with some of the other low tax havens such as Cyprus and Gibraltar.

The treaties provide for low withholding taxes on dividends and royalties paid from countries such as Malta, Norway, the US and the UK.

There is also an exchange on information agreement with the US.

The US-Barbados double tax treaty is often used to hold US property without being subject to US estate tax. This is due to the ability of Barbadian companies to hold shares in US property companies whilst avoiding US estate duty.

You could therefore live in a third country such as the UK and use the Barbadian tax treaty to obtain these benefits. Note that you would then need to consider your home country's tax rules (for example, the UK would then bring the US property into your estate if you were resident/domiciled there).

Celebrity Spotting

If you want to mingle with the rich and famous, Barbados is likely to be right up your street, as many celebrities either visit or have properties there.

It's known as a wealthy, well developed place (it has one of the highest literacy rates in the world) and unlike some of the other tax havens you'll see plenty of expensive cars (Jaguars, BMWs and Mercedes) if you visit.

The cost of living is very high, so don't consider moving there unless you have a lot of disposable income. But on the plus side, there are plenty of luxury properties available, the beaches are superb and crime is pretty low (except for burglary). All in all Barbados offers a very good standard of living, but at a price.

Barbadian companies are also subject to local taxes. In fact they are taxed pretty highly. Therefore unless there are special reasons (for example, tax treaty benefits) for using a Barbadian company these would not be at the top of most lists.

A Barbados resident company (one that is either incorporated in Barbados or is controlled from there) is taxed on its worldwide income. There is no 'domicile' rule as there is for individuals, so companies would be subject to a corporate tax rate of 37.5%.

If you did want to incorporate a company in Barbados, you'd be better off looking at a Barbadian IBC. There's a special IBC regime, which is used mainly by offshore trading companies (note not investment companies) which allows a reduced rate of corporation tax payable, often as low as 1% -2.5%.

Who Can Use Barbados to Save Tax?

Although the income tax is punitive, especially when compared with other offshore centres, in practice someone becoming resident in Barbados can easily make use of the non-Barbadian domicile rule to exempt all overseas sources of income.

Added to this is the fact that there is no capital gains tax, making Barbados a useful jurisdiction for individuals who want to cut their CGT bills when disposing of overseas assets. It also has some limited double tax treaties in place which could be effective in reducing withholding taxes.

If you're considering buying a home over there, property is available to non-Barbadians without any major restrictions (no need to get a licence like in Anguilla).

One point to note is that mortgage financing would not be available in Barbados to non-Barbadians. Therefore you'll either need to have the cash or arrange an offshore mortgage.

As for the level of property prices, they tend to be higher than the British Virgin Islands but not as high as Bermuda. You're looking at paying between £500,000 and £750,000 for a great four-bedroom beachfront property.

BELIZE

Belize is an independent country close to Mexico. Just like Barbados there is no capital gains tax or inheritance tax but there is income tax... and it can be pretty steep. The tax rate for employees can be as high as 45% and there are social security contributions on top of that.

Belize also has a special tax rule for individuals who are resident but not domiciled there: you only pay tax on income derived in Belize. This therefore exempts from tax most immigrants who usually keep their money invested offshore.

It's mainly individuals actually working in Belize who end up paying income tax.

Of course, it's not just the tax environment that needs to be considered. You would also need to consider whether Belize is the kind of place you would want to live.

As far as tax havens go it's undoubtedly one of the least developed and should only really be considered if you want a quiet life in a quiet backwater. The standard of living is relatively low and you'll be hard pushed to find a McDonald's or Burger King!

You can get your favourite western products but you'll pay through the nose for them.

Buying a property in Belize is pretty straightforward and there are no real restrictions on foreigners. Compared with other tax havens some property is dirt cheap. You can pick up a reasonable two-bedroom oceanfront apartment for just £50,000.

Given its growing reputation as a drug-trafficking centre, Belize is not usually thought of as the place to go if you want to escape crime. However, the country does have pretty stiff anti-drug laws and the problem tends to be confined to the major cities, which many expats would avoid in any case.

Local Belize companies pay corporation tax at the rate of 25%. However, if you're thinking about using an offshore entity you won't be using a 'standard' Belizean company. Instead you'll be using a Belizean international business company (IBC). This is exempt from all forms of tax in Belize.

It's not an ideal place for an offshore holding company due to the lack of double tax treaties with other countries (there are only treaties with the UK, Sweden, Denmark, some Caribbean countries and Austria) and is often used by offshore nominee or recharging companies.

How to Get a Residence Permit

One of the benefits of Belize is that it has pretty lax residence requirements and there are some established programmes that effectively let you buy your way in.

There is also a special programme for retirees in terms of which you can get permanent residence provided you are aged at least 45, can support yourself by earning at least $2,000 per month, and spend at least part of the year in Belize.

Of course the aim behind this is to encourage foreigners to bring in their cash to boost the local economy and from the immigrant's perspective, taking into account the low property prices and the low income threshold, it does offer an excellent opportunity to establish a tax haven lifestyle at a minimal initial cost.

You can also establish residence by investing more than $25,000 (for example, by buying a property in Belize) and provided you have income exceeding $1,000 per month (for a couple) the authorities would typically grant you residence.

BERMUDA

Everyone knows that Bermuda is a beautiful place. However, it's also attractive from a tax perspective. There is no:

- Income tax
- Capital gains tax

There are, however, some taxes for employees (including social security), property taxes and a form of stamp duty for Bermudian assets held at death. The social security contributions will only affect you if you want to get a job there. You'll be looking at paying 4.5% of your salary to the Government as well as a fixed weekly sum of about $20.

If you own property in Bermuda you'll be subject to property tax. This is based on the 'annual rental value', which is a notional figure, or the actual rent, whichever is the higher. The rates are low (usually around 0.5%).

There is also stamp duty on death which will be due if you own Bermudian assets at the date of death (rates are 5% or 10% dependent on the value of the assets).

Another plus is that there are no sales taxes so all in all the taxes are pretty low and it certainly looks like a good offshore option.

For Brits, Bermuda has the advantage of a strong British culture but it's also attractive due to the subtropical climate, which makes it mild for most of the year, although it can get very hot in summer. The island is also famous for its pink beaches.

Crime is certainly lower than most of the US or Europe but is growing, particularly in the back streets of the capital.

A word of caution – the cost of living is known to be extremely high (possibly double what you're used to) and the property prices are exorbitant. It will cost you about $1 million for an average house in Bermuda and well over $2.5 million for a luxury detached property.

However, buying a property out there is not straightforward. If you're non-Bermudian, the authorities impose some pretty hefty restrictions because owning a property in Bermuda gives you certain rights to come and go freely.

Firstly, you can only buy property from non-Bermudians, and secondly you will be limited to the type of property you can acquire. The Bermudian authorities don't want foreigners pricing the locals out of the property market, so you can only acquire a house that has an annual rental value of at least $126,000 or a condominium in a designated development.

So realistically you'd need to buy a property for at least $1 million. In addition you have to apply for a licence from the Bermudian immigration authorities, which is basically designed to check your background to keep out 'undesirables'.

Last but not least, you'll also need to pay a special property 'tax' on the purchase of your property at a whopping 22% of the cost if you're non-resident. This on its own is enough to prevent many people buying Bermudian property.

As such, actually obtaining residence in Bermuda is very difficult, and although you can get a right to live there by buying a property, actually getting a residence permit is notoriously difficult.

Setting Up an Offshore Company in Bermuda

Bermuda has a massive slice of the offshore company market (it has over 12,000 international companies) and some of the big FTSE and Fortune 100 companies have offshore holding companies incorporated there.

It's particularly popular with US companies given its geographic location. However, of more importance is the fact that it offers tax exemptions to companies incorporated under special exempt and overseas company provisions.

It's also a pretty well developed country with excellent communications and professional services and offers excellent political stability.

One of the main reasons for the number of offshore companies in Bermuda, though, is because of the Captive Insurance regulations.

Bermuda is a huge captive insurance market. Essentially captive insurance allows companies to 'self insure' their own liabilities and is a popular form of tax planning to secure a tax deduction for insurance premiums and roll-up cash tax free in Bermuda.

Note that, like the Bahamas, Bermuda has signed an Information Exchange Agreement (IEA) with the US and therefore any US citizens could find the IRS obtaining info on any interest earned on a Bermudian bank account. This would not apply to other tax authorities and banking secrecy would be paramount, unless there was evidence of criminal activities.

Note that a plus for Bermuda at the moment is that it is excluded from the impact of the EU Savings Tax Directive.

THE BRITISH VIRGIN ISLANDS (BVI)

The British Virgin Islands are one of the most famous tax havens thanks to being featured in numerous novels and films. This is also where you'll find Richard Branson's very own Necker island.

However, you may be surprised to know that the BVI fall into the 'low tax' as opposed to 'no tax' category.

In the British Virgin Islands there is no:

- Capital gains tax
- Inheritance tax
- Sales tax

Just like Barbados the main tax residents have to pay is income tax. There are also stamp duties and property taxes.

BVI residents pay income tax on their worldwide earnings (with double tax relief for any overseas tax paid if there's a double tax treaty).

Non-residents pay BVI income tax only on income arising or received in the BVI.

You'll be classed as a resident in the BVI if you are there for more than six months during the year.

The income tax rates are still pretty low when compared with other Western countries and there is a top rate of 20%. However, that's still a lot more than the nil-tax havens and if you've got significant income, the BVI probably won't be at the top of your list.

Of course if you want to escape capital gains tax or inheritance tax the BVI could still be an attractive place to go.

The climate in the BVI is generally hot, with an average temperature of 85 degrees. It's a beach lovers' paradise with some beautiful beachfront properties available.

Accommodation is of good quality and generally cheaper than the Cayman Islands and Bermuda. You're probably looking at paying between $500,000 and $750,000 for a beautiful beachfront residence.

But before you can buy property you'll need to obtain permission from the BVI authorities (known as a 'Non-Belongers Land Holding License').

The cost of living is high but less than Bermuda and slightly less than the Caymans (much the same as the UK, in fact). Crucially, crime is very low.

BVI companies are very popular. They have recently got rid of a 15% corporate tax in favour of a payroll tax. Under the new system, employers pay 6% payroll tax, while small businesses (defined as those employing less than seven people and with a payroll of less than $150,000 per year) pay tax at a reduced rate of 2%. So if you use the offshore company as an overseas investment company or for recharging there could well be no tax payable in the British Virgin Islands.

The BVI uses the same rules as the UK to decide if a company is resident in the BVI or not. Any company that is incorporated there or is managed and controlled from there is treated as BVI resident.

The BVI is a popular choice for establishing offshore companies (usually IBCs). It has a number of advantages including:

- Easy access to and from the islands from North America and Europe. Telephone, internet and postal services are good (as you'd expect from one of the main offshore financial centres).

- The official language is English.

- The BVI has traditionally offered excellent privacy as IBCs can offer bearer shares whereby it's not necessary to disclose the beneficial ownership of companies to any person in the BVI.

Bearer shares allow you to keep details of your shareholding private as ownership of the shares passes simply by physical transfer. As such, if you wanted to keep your holding of a particular company private, bearer shares could be ideal.

Note that the BVI have now made changes to the bearer share regime so that the name of the beneficial owner would need to be provided to certain 'custodians' such as certain financial institutions. They would, however, have to guarantee confidentiality.

Therefore whilst still allowing bearer shares, the privacy benefits have been restricted somewhat.

Overall the British Virgin Islands are an excellent base for establishing an offshore company and its use as a corporate tax haven is undoubtedly growing.

If you are looking to move permanently to the BVI there are no special residency or citizenship programmes. You could obtain residency by investing significant sums in the local economy or by marrying a local! There is no minimum investment stipulated and this would be a matter of negotiation with the BVI authorities.

THE CAYMAN ISLANDS

The Cayman Islands are one of the most famous tax havens and are a Hollywood favourite (this is where the Tom Cruise movie *The Firm* was filmed).

Located in the Caribbean they're an English-speaking dependent territory of the United Kingdom.

They give the impression of being a great hideaway where the rich and famous stash their millions free of tax. But just how true is this?

Well, the Cayman Islands certainly appear to offer the traditional benefits of a tax haven since they currently have no:

- Income tax or corporation tax
- Capital gains tax
- Inheritance tax or other estate taxes.

The Government raises its revenue from customs duties, stamp duty and annual company fees.

Beaches are magnificent and if you do move there you can enjoy an excellent standard of living. In fact residents have the highest standard of living in the Caribbean.

The cost of living is high (roughly 20% higher than the US) but certainly less than Bermuda and, as always, much will depend on the type of lifestyle you lead.

Note if you work there you can expect higher wages than in other Caribbean destinations (such as the BVI) to take account of the higher cost of living.

Property is pretty pricey as it's a prime location, although you can pick up some hurricane-damaged beachfront property at knock down prices. I've seen some beachfront property going for $500,000, which for the Caymans is dirt cheap! For top-quality beachfront properties you're looking at paying between $3 million and $4 million!

The fact that the islands were hit by a hurricane in 2004 may put a lot of people off, although the last major natural disaster was in 1932.

The Caymans are known to be extremely safe and whilst there is some petty crime (for example, pick pocketing) more serious crime is practically non-existent.

The Caymans' position as one of the world's top tax havens is supported by the fact that it is the largest offshore banking centre in the world with over 600 banks. The Cayman Islands are also home to some big trust businesses.

There are a number of different business entities you can set up here, with each having different formation rules. The Caymans provide for exempt companies, trusts and exempt limited partnerships which offer a 50-year Certificate of Tax Exemption against any future Caymans taxation. This is particularly popular as it provides an element of security to any would-be investor.

The Caymans are also well known for their confidentiality (always important for a tax haven) and the prevailing attitude is to protect confidentiality wherever possible.

A potential blot on the landscape is the Information Exchange Agreement (IEA) signed with the US. The agreement specifies that the Cayman Islands will share information with the US Government to help it trace financial criminals. The EU Savings Tax Directive will also apply.

This certainly dents the Caymans' reputation for secrecy. Under the IEA, provided the US Government has suspicion that a criminal offence has been committed it can request access to Cayman bank accounts. The IEA will also apply to civil investigations from 2006.

The Caymans therefore effectively ripped up their previous policy of non-disclosure and, given the appropriate circumstances, they will give information on the beneficial ownership of offshore companies and trusts where US residents or citizens are involved.

Of course this is only usually an issue if as a US resident (or citizen) you are not declaring your offshore income to the US IRS – which you should be.

As with most of the Caribbean tax havens, if you want to get residence there you'll need to prove that you won't be a drain on the local economy. This means you must have sufficient income or cash to support yourself and your family. Generally you'll also need to invest at least $180,000 in property or a business.

Given its low-tax status the Caymans are often used as a 'pit stop' for wealthy individuals emigrating to the United States. Typically they stop off in tax havens such as this and transfer assets to offshore companies or trusts before becoming US resident and subject to US taxes on their worldwide income and capital gains.

The Caymans have a number of advantages that have helped establish its reputation as an offshore centre, including:

- Excellent political stability
- No exchange controls and funds can be moved freely in or out
- Traditionally watertight confidentiality laws (although these have now been slightly eroded)
- Close proximity to the US
- Excellent communications
- Sophisticated legal, accounting and banking services

Cayman 'exempt' companies are also attractive as they allow for bearer shares and the use of nominee shareholders. These allow you to keep holdings of Cayman companies private. Nominee shareholders in particular are intended to disguise the true ownership of a company.

The downside is that it will generally cost you more to incorporate an IBC in the Caymans than in other jurisdictions such as Costa Rica, St Kitts Nevis or Mauritius. You're looking at paying between $3,000 and $4,000 to form a Cayman IBC, whereas a Costa Rican IBC could be formed for half the cost.

THE COOK ISLANDS

This is one of the lesser-known tax havens. The Cook Islands are extremely isolated geographically, located half way between New Zealand and Hawaii. The population is a mere 14,000!

It's not a nil-tax haven. Income tax is payable by those residing and working on the islands and is levied on a sliding scale with rates of 20%, 25% and 30%.

In terms of companies a resident company would be subject to tax of 20% on its worldwide profits.

There is VAT of 12.5% and there is also stamp duty. The Cook Islands have no double tax treaties.

Doesn't sound too good? Well I'd agree, except for the fact that offshore companies and trusts do not pay any taxes except for stamp duty.

There are about 15,000 offshore entities and the sector has been growing quite rapidly in recent years. Confidentiality is tight, except in cases of criminal activity, which does not include tax crime.

In addition, there is no capital gains tax, inheritance tax or wealth tax.

All in all, the Cook Islands is a useful place to base an offshore company but most people would not want to become resident there. Not only is it in the middle of nowhere, personal tax rates (except capital gains tax) are quite high.

If you did want to live there, you'd have to drastically change your way of life. As you'd expect it's a very simple lifestyle revolving around the beach and most people are incredibly laid back.

You won't be eating your usual produce and would need to adapt to the local diet, although other products can be imported from New Zealand. There are no cash machines on the island, although there are a couple of banks. There are some fine restaurants, particularly on the main island (Rarotonga). As you'd expect, crime is very low and the weather is warm pretty much all year round (with a rainy season from November to March).

As a non-resident foreigner you wouldn't be able to buy land in the Cook Islands. You'd have to rent a property and if you want a lease in excess of five years you'll have to get permission from the island's authorities.

If you want to become a permanent resident (you would then be able buy property) you need to either marry a local, gain local employment and live there for five years, or invest in a local company or business (the amounts vary from NZ$500,000 to NZ$1 million which is approximately US$330,000 to US$670,000).

Generally speaking it's difficult to get permanent residence there, particularly compared with other jurisdictions that offer much easier residency requirements.

COSTA RICA

Costa Rica is a Central American tax haven, located between Panama and Nicaragua.

In tax terms Costa Rica is highly attractive as it taxes on the basis of *territoriality*. Remember Barbados and the UK, which only tax overseas income of non-domiciliaries if the cash is brought into the country?

Well the territoriality principle takes this one step further and simply doesn't tax overseas income.

This principle of territoriality is the key aspect of the Costa Rican tax regime and only income earned within Costa Rica is subject to tax.

So provided a resident locates any income-producing assets outside Costa Rica, there is no tax payable. Remember though that any locally earned income, for example from a trade carried on from Costa Rica could be subject to local taxes at rates of up to 25%.

There is also no capital gains tax in Costa Rica. The authorities can apply income tax to some capital gains although if you dispose of property (or even shares) this will not apply.

It's really only gains made by businesses on the sale of trading assets that are be subject to income tax.

In terms of lifestyle, it's probably the most expensive country in Central America, but that doesn't mean you can't live there cheaply. The sales tax of 13% bumps up the cost of goods but utility bills and the cost of local products are cheap – it tends to be only imported goods that are very expensive.

Communications are very good with an excellent telephone system and internet access and the climate is mild most of the year.

Central America has a poor reputation in terms of crime and personal security and although Costa Rica is probably the safest, you would still need to be vigilant.

Property prices are very low and Costa Rica has been touted as one of the next property investment hot spots.

Unfortunately there is no finance available to foreigners and therefore you'd either need to arrange this in another country or become a resident.

Property is a fair bit cheaper than some of the other more cosmopolitan tax havens. In fact one opportunity I saw recently was 800 acres of rainforest, including a beach and a couple of large houses for approximately £800,000.

If you're after a reasonably priced beachfront property this may be a good place to buy as you can pick up a property for about $100,000! However, most quality beachfront homes go for over $500,000.

In terms of establishing yourself as a resident in Costa Rica, the authorities do offer specific residency programmes that allow you to easily establish yourself as a resident.

One of the best schemes is the 'rentista' scheme which applies to foreigners with guaranteed income. In order to gain residency under this, you'll need to show that your investment income will generate at least $1,000 per month for a single person, or $2,000 per month for a married couple and that you live in Costa Rica for at least six months during the year. You'll then be entitled to live in Costa Rica and take advantage of the tax exemption for your non-Costa Rican income.

Domestic companies face a high tax bill, with a top corporation tax rate of 30%, and there are also high social security charges that could apply. However, Costa Rican companies are still popular as the territoriality principle applies to companies as well as individuals. Therefore offshore companies carrying out no activities in Costa Rica, or holding no Costa Rican assets, can avoid local taxes altogether.

In addition, the country has no double tax treaties but does have an exchange of information treaty with the US.

All in all, Costa Rica offers good opportunities for individuals looking to shelter offshore income and gains and allows you to establish yourself offshore at a reasonable price.

CYPRUS

Cyprus is one of Europe's key tax havens and is only a four-hour flight from the UK.

It's a popular destination for those wanting to avoid capital gains tax and is becoming increasingly popular as a home for setting up offshore structures.

One of the key benefits of Cyprus is that it has double-tax treaties with 27 other countries, including most major Western 'high-tax' countries and most Central and Eastern European states.

This is unusual for a tax haven and means that Cyprus is a very good choice for holding and investment companies.

Income tax rates vary from 20% to 30% although there is a special 5% rate for pensioners.

However, the beauty of Cyprus is in the exemptions. All of the following are tax free:

- Interest received by individuals
- 50% of interest income of companies
- Dividends
- Profits of permanent establishments carrying on a trade abroad
- Profits from the sale of shares
- Income from employment services provided abroad to a non-resident employer

Cyprus also offers an attractive capital gains tax (CGT) regime. CGT is levied at the rate of 20% on gains arising from the disposal of land and property *situated in Cyprus* or the disposal of shares in a company (excluding shares of listed companies) which owns land or property situated in Cyprus.

Therefore if a Cypriot resident owns property overseas there is no CGT payable in Cyprus on the disposal. So a disposal of UK property would not be subject to Cypriot tax if you are a Cypriot resident.

Cyprus has gained increased prominence due to its treaties with Eastern European countries. These enable a Cyprus legal entity to extract profits from Eastern European countries at a reduced tax rate or with no tax payable at all. This is thanks to the nil (or low) rates of withholding taxes on dividends, interest and royalties laid out in the treaties.

Given that many Eastern European countries are seeing increased inward investment, the interest in Cyprus companies (in order to take advantage of these low withholding taxes) is likely to continue growing.

Cyprus is a good choice for Europeans as it's not too far from home but offers an excellent low-tax environment with a low cost of living. In fact it's one of the cheapest countries in Europe and this is a big advantage for potential emigrants, particularly pensioners.

It's a totally different environment when compared with the Caribbean tax havens which are, by and large, developing countries albeit with some highly developed areas.

Cyprus is a well developed country with excellent communication and transport links and a good choice of restaurants, department stores and everything else to make it a home from home. (In other words you won't have to go without your favourite snacks and other home comforts!)

Weather wise, from March to November you'll be looking at glorious sunshine. The rest of the year will be cooler and there'll probably be a fair bit of rain in January and February – although after experiencing 40 degrees every day you'll probably be glad for the change.

All in all, it's a Mediterranean climate with a lot of sunshine. Cyprus is also a good choice for parents with young children as the schools are generally good and you can choose between state and private schools.

The crime rate is very low, particularly compared with other western European states, although it is increasing.

It's also easier for European residents to establish residence in Cyprus now that it's part of the EU. In order to be classed as a Cypriot resident you need to spend at least 183 days in the country during the tax year.

Cyprus property has been booming in the last few years and there are still some great investment opportunities. While the prices aren't as cheap as in parts of the Caribbean or even other tax havens such as Malta, they are cheaper than the UK, US and Canada, and you can get a nice place for $250,000.

Pensioners in particular are in a tax privileged position in Cyprus. This is particularly the case for UK retirees as the tax treaty ensures that any UK pensions are taxed in Cyprus rather than the UK. Given that Cyprus has a special low 5% tax rate for pensions it's no surprise that many well informed senior citizens are moving there.

As for companies, Cyprus imposes corporation tax on companies that carry on business or have an office or place of business (permanent establishment) in Cyprus. Cyprus now has a 10% corporate tax rate, which applies to all companies and there is an extra 2% charge on salary bills. This gives Cyprus one of the lowest corporation tax rates in Europe.

Unlike the UK and the US the shareholders are not liable to income tax on dividends when profits are extracted from a company.

It's also worth noting that a number of the treaties have tax-sparing provisions. A tax-sparing provision means that, even if income is tax free in Cyprus, it can still be given as a tax credit in the other country as if it had already been paid (in other words, you get a tax credit without incurring the tax charge).

These tax-sparing provisions are usually given by developed countries to developing countries to encourage investment and economic development. The types of situations where this will be given is where tax is paid in the UK or Canada on interest on a loan that is used for economic development in Cyprus.

In summary, Cyprus is one of the top tax havens for UK pensioners and anyone wanting to wipe out a big capital gains tax bill. Its popularity has increased due to the lifestyle, low cost of living and booming property prices.

Cypriot offshore companies are also popular, particularly for investment in Eastern Europe and holding companies.

DUBAI

Dubai has become an increasingly popular destination for UK investors looking to cash in on the local property boom or earn a tax-free salary.

Dubai is a nil-tax haven for individuals. There is no:

- Personal income tax
- Capital gains tax
- Inheritance tax
- Sales tax

It therefore holds up well against the other tax haven states. As a bonus it also has about 40 tax treaties, which is rare for a tax haven, although these tend to mainly benefit Dubai companies allowing reduced withholding taxes on dividends.

Unless you're a visitor from certain Arab states, you'll need to get a visa. For example, if you are going there on holiday, the tour operator will usually get you a 14- or 30-day tourist visa. Those thinking of snapping up some investment property will be happy to know that the purchase of a freehold property entitles you to apply for a residence permit giving you free entry and exit from Dubai.

Much has been written about the Dubai property revolution. However, you should bear in mind that you will not have free rein to buy property wherever you choose. Non-residents can only buy property inside special zones and are mainly restricted to new developments.

Prices are still reasonable and you could pick up a nice two-bed apartment for £70,000.

A concern of more cautious property investors is how the local succession laws will apply to their property if they die. This is a complex area but there are specific forced succession rules that are likely to be different to those in most European countries.

For this reason a lot of expats opt to own Dubai property via an offshore company. The benefit of this is that the shares in the company can usually be transferred in accordance with your home country's rules of succession.

In terms of lifestyle, Dubai is known to be an excellent place to live with a very low crime rate and very good schools and medical facilities, although you'll probably need to pay for a private international school for your children.

It's well known for its shopping facilities and, apart from over 50 large shopping centres, there are also the local markets or souks where you can pick up bargains (if you're prepared to haggle!).

Hi-tech goods such as computers and other home electronic devices can be bought at bargain prices. The overall cost of living is also very reasonable (you can pick up a kebab for just 50p).

Remember that Dubai is still a Muslim country and as such you would need to be mindful of the rules. Having said that, it's fair to say that Dubai is probably the most Western of the United Arab Emirates (as you'd expect with over 50% of the population being expats) and therefore the rules are not as strict as in other Muslim states.

Therefore you can still obtain alcohol in restaurants and hotels and, although Arabic is the official language, most people speak English.

As well as the personal tax benefits, Dubai is becoming of more importance as a home for offshore companies.

It's certainly not cheap to set up a company there (you're looking at about $5,000 to incorporate and annual renewal fees are in the region of $2,500) but the benefit of course is the zero tax rates. Note when forming a company you'd be looking to set it up in one of the special 'zones' available to expats. The Jebel Ali free zone is the most popular.

As well as the tax benefits, a Dubai-registered company offers very good privacy and confidentiality, particularly given the fact that Dubai has no information exchange treaties. As a result Dubai companies are favoured in asset protection schemes.

A common technique, particularly for e-commerce businesses, is to form an offshore company such as a Panama or British Virgin Islands IBC and to register it in one of the free trade zones. The Dubai Internet City (DIC) is a free trade zone specifically for e-commerce businesses.

This would then guarantee no Dubai taxes for 50 years.

The combination of Dubai and a good offshore jurisdiction such as the British Virgin Islands would ensure that there would be no disclosure of shareholders and only limited disclosure of the directors (potentially only nominee directors) so reinforcing the asset protection benefits.

Overall Dubai is a good option, particularly for property investors interested in the potential returns. The downside of course is that it's located in a politically sensitive area of the world. While the United Arab Emirates has not been the subject of any significant religious tension, this is not to say that this may not change in the future.

EASTERN EUROPE

Maybe not your first choice of tax havens, the countries of Eastern Europe are certainly worth knowing about given the rapid economic growth being enjoyed and the flood of investors looking for bargain properties.

Many of the Eastern European states levy what is known as a flat-rate tax. This is perhaps the most simple of all taxes as everyone's income is taxed at the same rate. The thinking is that, if the rate is set low enough, most people won't mind coughing up and the black economy will shrink – resulting in greater tax collections than before.

Having said this, there are only a couple of Eastern European states that offer tax rates as low as many of the tax havens you'll read about in this book. Below are the income tax rates in some of the Eastern European countries:

- Estonia   23%
- Latvia   25%
- Lithuania   33%
- Serbia   20%
- Ukraine   13%
- Slovakia   19%
- Romania   16%
- Russia   13%

There are also Eastern European countries that levy tax on a normal 'progressive basis' (in other words, the more you earn, the higher the tax rate). So countries like Hungary can tax at rates of up to 38%, Croatia at up to 45%, and Bosnia up to 25%.

Based on the above, the only really low tax states are Russia, Ukraine and potentially, Romania.

In terms of capital gains, most of these states class gains as additional income, however there are some specific rules, particularly in relation to land and property disposals, that are worth remembering. These could be of use to budding overseas property investors who want to make profits in emerging markets.

Croatia has high rates of income tax but taxes gains on land at a standard rate of 25%. However, there is a tax exemption if the property is either your main residence or if you've owned it for at least three years.

Russia classes gains as additional income (which would be subject to the 13% income tax rate for residents) but will exempt gains completely if you've owned the property for at least three years.

Slovakia exempts property gains if the property is either your main residence (for at least two years) or if you've owned the property for at least five years.

Lithuania exempts Lithuanian property if you've owned it for at least three years.

Russia and most of the East European countries also do not have any inheritance tax.

Therefore, on the plus side, Russia looks good in terms of both low overall tax rates and the potential exemption for property gains.

As with most of the Eastern European states, Russia adopts the usual method of determining your residence status. Anyone actually in Russia for more than 183 days in the calendar year is considered a resident for tax purposes. You would then need to file a Russian personal income tax return.

Entry to and from Russia is very tightly controlled and you'd need to get yourself a visa from a Russian Embassy. There are different types of visa available (tourist visas, business visas etc) and each visa will have different qualifying conditions and allow you to spend a specified period in Russia.

The business visa is generally preferred as this allows you to spend up to 12 months in the country.

In order to live there on even a semi-permanent basis you would need to get a residence permit. These are difficult to obtain, unless you were born in Russia or are married to a Russian citizen. The first step would be to get a temporary visa, which could then be upgraded to a permanent visa.

All in all if you are looking to get a foot in the door in a developing economy, Russia may be an option and the low taxes would be an added bonus.

GIBRALTAR

Gibraltar is one of the well-established European tax havens. It's a self governing but dependent territory of the United Kingdom.

Gibraltar is a 'low-tax' haven rather than a 'no-tax' haven.

There's no capital gains tax, wealth tax or VAT but, as you've probably guessed, there is income tax... and it can be quite high, with the top rate being 45%.

You'll be resident in Gibraltar if you spend more than 183 days there in any 12-month period. You will then be subject to Gibraltar tax on your worldwide income.

However, if you're moving to Gibraltar to exploit the tax-saving opportunities you should be looking at obtaining High Net Worth Individual (HNWI) status.

This will allow you to massively reduce your income tax liability.

The main purpose of the HNWI provisions is to encourage wealthy people to live in Gibraltar. A person who has not been resident in Gibraltar for the last five years can apply for this HNWI status.

Expat executives and people with specialist skills may be able to obtain a similar limitation on their total tax payable. This is a highly attractive status to achieve and is well worth considering if you're looking for a low-tax environment within the EU.

The beauty of this status is that it allows you to obtain residence status in Gibraltar and avoid paying tax elsewhere.

You'll then get a residence card from the Gibraltar Government which will help to justify not paying tax in your country of origin (for example, the UK).

HNWIs are entitled to reside in Gibraltar together with their spouses and children and they will all obtain Gibraltar ID cards/residence permits allowing free movement in and out of Gibraltar.

In order to qualify there are, as you'd expect, a number of conditions that need to be satisfied.

- You must not have been a resident of Gibraltar in the preceding five years.

- You must have a property in Gibraltar available for your exclusive use for at least seven months during the tax year.

- You need to actually live in the Gibraltar property for at least 30 days during the year.

- You must have private health insurance.

- You must have enough income to support yourself and your family.

- You won't be able to trade in Gibraltar but for most HNWIs this is not an issue. You could, however, telecommute with another offshore company.

What do you get for satisfying all these conditions? Well essentially Gibraltar will only tax a proportion of your income. The maximum is roughly £50,000, so any income over this is tax free.

There is, however, a minimum amount of tax payable which is set at approximately £14,000.

There can be massive tax savings for a high earner and it's aimed directly at these individuals as you'll need to get a banker's reference to vouch for the fact that your net assets are in excess of £2 million.

Also remember that, as well as there being no capital gains tax in Gibraltar, a HNWI is also exempt from estate duty.

If you want to apply for HNWI status you would need to make an application to the Gibraltar authorities and submit the non-refundable application fee of £1,000 and two references, one from a banker. (Note that officially the HNWI is now known as a 'Category 2' individual.)

Another advantage of the HNWI status is that only income actually remitted or received in Gibraltar is counted towards the

£50,000 taxable income. You'll therefore find that most emigrants will restrict their flow of money to Gibraltar so that their taxable income is much less than £50,000.

Income tax is charged on most types of income including trading income, investment income and employment income and although the maximum income tax rate under the HNWI provisions is the standard income tax rate of 45%, this could still be less than the tax you would pay in many of the industrialised countries, due to the limitation on the amount of income that is taxed.

Gibraltar is popular with wealthy UK expats because it is so British and relatively easy to move to from the UK.

It has a nice Mediterranean climate and the crime rate is very low. On the downside it is very densely populated (less than six square kilometres in area but it has over 30,000 people living there).

High-quality property is notoriously expensive. This is due to a combination of high demand and limited supply due to the shortage of space. In addition, if you're looking for a luxury villa with grounds you're likely to be disappointed. Most of the developments are apartments.

Having said that, there is a broad spread of property available. One website specialising in Gibraltar real estate has beachfront studio flats going for just £75,000 and a six-bedroom villa overlooking the Straits of Gibraltar going for £1.1 million.

In between that you can pick up three-bedroom apartments for £175,000 and four-bedroom apartments for £250,000. A three-bedroom house in a gated estate with a private garden and communal swimming pool could cost about £700,000.

On the plus side if you're a British citizen you are allowed to live and work in Gibraltar without obtaining a residence permit. If you aren't British but are from an EU country, you'll need to get a residence permit (and show you have sufficient income to support yourself). If you're not from the EU it is much more difficult as you'll need to get a work permit first before applying for a residence permit.

As for companies, the main tax is income tax, which was traditionally set at 35%, except for certain exempt or non-resident companies. However, Gibraltar has introduced a new 0% rate of corporation tax for all companies but with additional company return fees and special taxes on payroll and for property companies. These changes are being questioned by the EU commission and it may take a number of years before the issue is resolved.

Gibraltar also has an attractive trust regime. Trusts created by non-residents that generate overseas income are exempt from Gibraltar income tax.

Gibraltar has a lot to offer on many different fronts: low taxes (especially if you obtain HNWI status), a beautiful climate, close proximity to most European countries, British culture and reasonable property prices compared with some of the more exclusive tax havens.

GUERNSEY & JERSEY

These lovely islands form part of the Channel Islands and are located between England and France.

They are both self-governing British Crown dependencies and famous for their tax-haven status. The islands are particularly attractive to people in the UK who want to lose their UK resident status (for example, to avoid capital gains tax) without moving too far from home.

Apart from having no capital gains tax, there is also no inheritance tax or VAT in the Channel Islands.

The main tax that residents have to pay is income tax, which is set at a flat rate of 20%. Although reasonably low, if you have substantial income there are other tax havens that may be more attractive.

Property prices are quite steep compared with many regions of the UK but more reasonable than many parts of the South East.

I've seen one-bedroom apartments in the centre of St Helier going for just £85,000 and two-bedroom apartments for £150,000 – possibly ideal buy-to-let investments.

A two-bedroom semi-detached house will usually cost around £300,000 but I've seen five-bedroom properties needing refurbishment going for the same price.

At the better end of the market I've seen a beautiful three-bedroom granite house in St Brelade, built in the 1880s, going for £750,000, complete with its own swimming pool and secluded garden.

It's essential to point out that it is almost impossible for most people to obtain permanent residence in Jersey. One of the main factors the powers that be take into account is how much tax you are likely to contribute. Only multimillionaires are considered and preferably those with income of at least £500,000. There are also restrictions on property ownership

However, there's nothing to stop you from setting up an offshore trust or company on the islands. Guernsey and Jersey offer an attractive offshore company regime. There are a number of different companies, which are each treated differently for tax purposes.

Resident companies pay full income tax on their worldwide income. However if you set up a Jersey International Business Company (IBC) this will only pay full income tax on income arising in Jersey.

There are also special 'exempt' companies that are similar to IBCs in that they only pay income tax on their income arising from a place of business in Jersey.

The standard rate of Jersey corporate income tax is 20% but for IBCs with Jersey income the rate is 30%. Jersey IBCs are also subject to a minimum annual tax liability of £1,200. Therefore they're really only of benefit if you undertake no business on the islands.

Both of the islands are beneficial as trust jurisdictions. The main benefit is that when the beneficiaries of a trust are non-resident, there is no local tax charged on foreign income and local bank interest. interest. This makes Channel Island trusts popular with UK residents.

The lack of double tax treaties reduces the attractiveness of the islands as a holding company destination. However if you're looking to avoid capital gains tax or just reduce income tax, either of the two would be a good choice.

In terms of security and stability they are, as you would expect, as good as it gets. Unfortunately there are no special regimes such as Gibraltar's HNWI scheme to enable income tax to be significantly reduced.

If you're looking for cheaper property prices and a more sedate way of life, the Channel Island of Alderney may be worth considering. It offers the same tax advantages as Jersey and Guernsey but is much smaller.

IRELAND

Ireland has traditionally been a popular retirement destination and is particularly attractive to writers and painters who don't have to pay a penny of tax on their royalties. Any budding artists out there should note, however, that the Irish taxman is looking at placing a limit on the income that is tax exempt, due to a number of Irish artists (such as the band U2) using the favourable regime to avoid massive sums in tax.

Ireland is certainly not one of the nil tax havens and would fall firmly in the low tax category. The Irish levy income tax and capital gains tax and there's also inheritance tax. The actual rate of income tax is 20% for income up to €32,000 and 42% above this.

These rates are quite high but there are tax benefits for individuals who are non-domiciled. Just as in the UK and Barbados, there's a clear distinction between a person's domicile and residence status for tax purposes.

In effect, a 'foreign' person resident in Ireland only needs to pay tax on income brought into Ireland.

You can therefore keep most of your income offshore and avoid paying any income tax.

In fact, if a suitable distinction is made between capital and subsequent income from capital before you take up permanent residence (such as using capital and income accounts – see Chapter 11) it may even be possible to live in Ireland almost completely tax free.

This favourable tax treatment is also available to Irish domiciled persons for a three-year period after returning to Ireland from a prolonged period of absence.

Ireland is also well known as a good base for international employees. The Irish tax rules do not tax Irish residents working outside Ireland on their overseas income, even if remitted.

As usual, your residence status for Irish tax purposes is determined by the number of days you spend in the country during the tax year.

You will be classed as Irish resident if:

- You spend 183 days or more in the country during the tax year, or

- You spend 280 days or more in Ireland over a period of two consecutive tax years. You will then be regarded as resident in Ireland for the second tax year.

(However if you spend 30 days or less in the country in either tax year, those days will not be taken into account when calculating if you have breached the 280-day limit.)

In other respects Ireland follows the standard rules and taxes resident and domiciled individuals on their worldwide income and non-residents only on their Irish income.

Ireland does have a capital gains tax which is levied at a rate of just 20%.

As for actually living and working there, Ireland offers excellent opportunities especially for EU nationals who don't need a residence or work permit. Residents of most non-EU countries (except for the US, Australia and Canada) will need a residence and work permit.

The climate is mild, the country has excellent transport and communication links and the level of crime, particularly violent crime, is low.

The overall cost of living is high, however this goes hand in hand with the high standard of living.

Property prices are reasonable in many parts of the country but astronomical in Dublin, which has enjoyed a property boom in recent years fuelled by low Eurozone interest rates.

Another reason why Ireland is a popular choice with EU expats is that there are no restrictions on the purchase of property (unlike many of the other tax havens).

The corporate tax regime is also one of the most attractive in the world thanks to a combination of low tax rates and lots of tax treaties which Irish resident companies can take advantage of.

Irish companies are taxed on trading income at a rate of just 12.5%. This only applies to trading income and the rate applied to non-trading income is 25%.

This is the second lowest rate of corporation tax in the EU (just behind Cyprus and the Isle of Man, which have a 10% corporation tax rate) and is one of the lowest in any developed economy in the world. So it's not surprising that Ireland's offshore sector has boomed.

Ireland has been a very popular alternative 'offshore' choice for many multinationals which have transferred some of their operations to Irish companies to reduce their overall effective tax rate.

Ireland therefore offers excellent tax-saving opportunities at both the corporate and personal level.

THE ISLE OF MAN

The Isle of Man (IOM) is located just off the west coast of England, approximately 70 miles from Liverpool.

In comparison with other tax havens it definitely falls into the 'low-tax' rather than no-tax category.

There are generous income tax allowances for individuals and married couples. For example, for a married couple, the first £17,000 of income is automatically tax free. The next £20,600 is taxed at 10%, with income above this taxed at just 18%.

To attract more 'high-net-worth individuals and active entrepreneurs' it was announced in the February 2006 Budget that the total tax payable will be capped: no resident will pay more than £100,000 in tax.

On the Isle of Man there is also no:

- Capital gains tax (CGT), or
- Inheritance tax

The island is therefore a good place to live if you want to avoid paying tax when you sell your property portfolio.

In comparison with many of the other tax havens, Manx tax exiles tend to be quite understated. You won't find a harbour full of expensive yachts or Ferraris parked on every street corner. The island is a lot more 'gritty' than some of the other boltholes of the rich and famous.

The IOM nevertheless offers a good quality of life provided you don't mind the cold. It has good education and health services and a very low crime rate. Violent crime in particular is low, as is car theft (it's difficult to get cars off an island).

Many potential emigrants would probably look further afield and for some it's difficult to see the attraction of a cold island off the coast of England, especially when there are tax havens offering much warmer climates and equally attractive tax laws.

However, the Isle of Man attracts more than its fair share of expats and over 50% of the population weren't actually born there – after all, it's close to the UK, easy to emigrate to and property prices are quite reasonable compared with other European tax havens.

At the top of the pile you'll find, for example, a large period country residence set in 12 acres with eight bedrooms and an indoor pool complex going for £1.4 million.

A bit lower down the scale, £500,000 will buy you a modern four-bedroom detached house with close to an acre of grounds and panoramic coastal and rural views.

For £375,000 you could buy a very pretty four-bedroom detached house in Douglas (the capital) with a secluded garden.

At the bottom of the ladder you'll find one-bedroom apartments for between £70,000 and £80,000 and two-bedroom apartments for £120,000 and modern three-bedroom semi-detached houses for just £165,000.

There are certainly bargains there for the taking (for example, a six-bedroom mid-terrace house in Douglas going for just £230,000)

The Isle of Man is extremely stable politically, as you'd expect given that it is a UK Crown dependency. The island does, however, run its own affairs and makes its own laws.

For UK expats, actually moving over there is pretty easy as well. There is unrestricted access for UK citizens and residents in the European Economic Area.

It has also recently been announced that a 0% rate of corporate tax for all companies (except banks) comes into force from April 2006. Prior to this companies have been subject to a tax rate of just 10% but if they could qualify for exempt or international company status they could earn income free of any local taxes.

This 0% corporate tax charge gives the Isle of Man the lowest corporate tax rate in Europe.

The Isle of Man is therefore a good choice for UK nationals wanting to escape high taxation but remain close to home. In addition, it's growing in popularity as a destination for e-commerce businesses to relocate to, due to its sound telecoms infrastructure and 100% broadband coverage.

LIECHTENSTEIN

Liechtenstein is a tiny landlocked country sandwiched between Switzerland and Austria with only 32,000 inhabitants.

The official language is German, although English and French are also spoken.

Unlike other tax havens, there are no special rules for offshore entities – in Liechtenstein everybody enjoys low taxes.

Note that I use the term 'low taxes'. There are still taxes, the most common one being income tax. There is also a type of wealth tax called the 'net worth tax' and VAT is levied on most goods and services.

Whether or not you have to pay tax in Liechtenstein depends on your residence status. You will be classed as resident if:

- You have a property there that you keep as a permanent residence, or

- You are living in Liechtenstein and either have a job or your own business there.

As with most countries, if you are deemed to be resident you are liable to pay tax on your worldwide income.

Income tax in Liechtenstein is payable on income from your job or business but because there is a wealth tax, there is no income tax on investment income (dividends, interest, rental income etc), provided the underlying assets have been subject to the wealth tax.

Any capital gains are also usually taxed as income, except for certain property disposals, which are taxed separately.

Any tax bill would be reduced by a variety of personal allowances and capital gains annual exemptions, which total between 5,000 and 11,000 Swiss Francs (between £2,000 and £5,000).

Unlike many countries that have a system of independent taxation, married couples are taxed jointly in Liechtenstein. The rate of income tax depends on the level of taxable income and also the area in which the taxpayer is resident.

The maximum marginal rate is approximately 18% on taxable income of approximately CHF180,000 (£80,000).

There is also a system of social security contributions and employees pay this at the rate of 4.3% of gross pay (although the self employed are punished and pay a rate of up to 11%).

The net worth tax is applied to your *net* assets (the market value of your total assets minus your liabilities). Assets include land and property, bank accounts, shares, valuables, works of art etc. Liabilities include debts etc.

When calculating the net worth tax charge, the first CHF20,000 of net assets is usually exempt with the balance taxed on a sliding scale, reaching a maximum marginal rate of about 0.9% on taxable net wealth of about CHF350,000 (£150,000).

Liechtenstein also has gift and estate taxes. Like many European countries the rate at which the gift tax is levied will vary depending on the relationship between the donor and the donee. Any gifts made to close family such as spouses or children are taxed at just 0.5%. Gifts to more remote family such as grandparents are taxed at 2%. The highest rate of 18% is reserved for gifts to non family and unconnected people. Since assets are left to spouses or children in most cases, the rate of inheritance tax would be minimal.

There are a variety of offshore entities that are used to take advantage of the low taxes. Liechtenstein is most famous for its 'Anstalt' and 'Stiftung'. The Anstalt is a unique form of legal structure with no members or shareholders. It is a separate entity with beneficiaries and provided it operates as an investment entity its income could be tax free.

The stiftung is essentially a Liechtenstein foundation (see Chapter 5 for more on the use of foundations). The Liechtenstein foundation was one of the first around and although more expensive than those available in other jurisdictions, is still popular with the very wealthy thanks to the high level of confidentiality and privacy offered.

Liechtenstein has strong bank secrecy and the EU Savings Tax Directive does apply. Information exchange only applies in cases of tax fraud and the like.

Liechtenstein has strong bank secrecy and it will only usually consider information exchange in cases of tax fraud and the like. It has, however, signed up to the EU Savings Tax Directive and will be applying a withholding tax rather than sharing information (for more about this directive see Chapter 9).

As far as living there is concerned, Liechtenstein is very scenic with some beautiful mountains and valleys. It's warm in summer but there's plenty of snow in winter. The cost of living is notoriously high.

As it's not part of the EU you'll need to get a residence permit if you want to live there. Although it's part of the European Economic Area (EEA), given its small size, residence permits are restricted.

You would need to apply direct to the Liechtenstein immigration authorities if you wanted to live or emigrate there and, as usual, they would want to identify your financial means and ability to support yourself and your family.

MALTA

Malta is situated in the Mediterranean, just below Sicily. It's not a well-known bolthole but offers some excellent tax breaks to individuals who want to establish themselves in a flexible low-tax haven 'on the cheap'.

The actual income-tax rates are very high, with all but the lowest-paid being taxed at 35%.

However, if you get classed as a 'permanent resident' the tax rates are much lower. You'll only be subject to 15% income tax on local income or overseas income that you bring into Malta.

It also offers the non domiciliary exemption (like the UK, Ireland and Barbados) so that only overseas income actually brought into Malta is taxed.

In addition, there is no capital gains tax when you sell overseas assets and there is no inheritance tax. So all in all it looks like a good rival to some of the other European low tax havens such as Cyprus, the Isle of Man and Ireland.

It's also worth noting that Malta has a fair number of double tax treaties, which can help to ensure that overseas income is only taxed in Malta.

The agreement with the UK, for example, can help to ensure that UK pensions are not subject to any tax in the UK and are taxed in Malta at just 15%. So Malta could be an attractive retirement destination.

Apart from the low tax rate, as a resident you'll also qualify for some tax-free allowances, worth approximately $6,000 to a married couple.

You can't use the domicile exemption to escape Maltese tax by keeping all your money out of the country as the Maltese authorities would want a minimum of 1,000 Maltese Lira (approximately $2,700) in tax each year.

However, even if you're an average earner, Malta still offers a great opportunity to slash your tax bill.

Another plus point is that acquiring permanent residence is not as difficult as in other tax havens. The Maltese Government is keen to attract foreign nationals to the island.

In order to be accepted, the first step is to satisfy the authorities that you have enough income or capital to support yourself.

You'll therefore need to have an annual income of at least $25,000 or have assets of at least $375,000.

You'll also need to show that you can bring at least $15,000 into the country each year and $2,500 for each of your dependants.

Your application also needs to be accompanied by character references.

I'm sure you'll agree that the above requirements are not that difficult to satisfy, especially when you take into account the likely tax benefits.

Once you receive your permanent residence permit, you'll have 12 months to either purchase an apartment for at least $75,000 or a house for $125,000 or rent a property for at least $4,500 per annum.

Aside from this, the requirements are very flexible, and you'll have completely free movement on and off the island.

The standard of living is very high with good schools and medical facilities (ranked fifth in the world by the World Health Organisation). The University of Malta has an excellent reputation and is open to the children of permanent residents.

The island boasts an excellent Mediterranean lifestyle, with good restaurants, a casino and golf resorts. The all-important crime rate is still very low, and you'll find plenty of locals leave their doors open, even when they go out.

Whilst is has a high standard of living, the cost of living is surprisingly low – lower than, for example, the UK, Spain, Portugal, France, Italy and Cyprus.

Property is not cheap but prices are pretty reasonable when compared with some other European destinations. A three-bedroom semi-detached villa with a large garden and country views can be picked up for about $342,000.

Bargains are also there for the taking. A one-bedroom maisonette with sea views can cost as little as $100,000.

At the other end of the scale, a four-bedroom detached seafront villa with a very large garden will cost about $1 million.

In terms of infrastructure, Air Malta provides flights to a broad selection of European destinations and the island has excellent broadband internet access.

Overall, Malta offers excellent benefits and should be given serious consideration by anyone wanting to live in a country with low tax rates and a Mediterranean way of life.

Malta has also been gaining increasing prominence as a jurisdiction to locate an offshore IBC. In Malta these companies are known as International Trading Companies.

When owned by non-Maltese residents, these companies are subject to the standard 35% tax rate but refunds are then given to reduce the effective tax rate to (usually) less than 5%.

Added to the fact that Malta has a big network of double tax treaties (including treaties with all EU members), means it can be another good choice to locate an offshore trading company.

MONACO

Located on the stunning French Riviera there is probably no tax haven more famous than Monaco.

In recent years the well-known British entrepreneur Philip Green has made full use of the favourable tax laws there to pay his Monaco-based wife hundreds of millions of pounds in tax-free dividends from UK companies.

There is no income tax or capital gains tax in Monaco – the main tax is a business profits tax that is levied on certain companies (but most expats structure their affairs so as to avoid it).

There is also inheritance tax but there are two major exemptions that limit its application in practice. Firstly, the tax is payable only on assets situated in Monaco and secondly the tax rate depends on how closely related the parties are. The closer the relationship, the lower the inheritance tax rate.

The rates payable are as follows:	Tax Rate
Wife, parents and children	0%
Brothers and sisters	8%
Uncles, aunts, nieces and nephews	10%
Other relatives	13%
Unrelated persons	16%

So assets left to a spouse or children can usually be transferred free of inheritance tax.

Monaco is well known as a playground of the rich and famous. It has gorgeous weather, exclusive shops and hotels and is a fantastically safe place to live.

Not only is there a large police force (something like one policeman for every 100 residents) but the entire principality is covered by CCTV.

As you'd expect, the standard of living is extremely high but so are living costs – you'll be looking at paying over £50 for just two cocktails in one of the swanky bars.

Buying a property in Monaco is simple in theory as no restrictions are placed on non-residents.

In practice most of the decent properties are far too expensive for the average expat.

Most of the residents live in apartments and the best of these go for several million euros. However, you can pick up a studio flat for around €600,000 – not a great solution for a couple with young children but possibly worth considering if you're free and single.

If you're after a decent villa or house in the principality, brace yourself for open-wallet surgery. You could end up paying as much as €15 million.

The real attraction of Monaco as a tax haven is its geographic location and lifestyle. Unlike many tax havens which are situated in the middle of nowhere, Monaco is only a short drive from several major European cities.

Access to banks and financial services is excellent, as you would expect given the number of mega-rich inhabitants.

Obtaining residence in Monaco is not as difficult as you might expect, provided you have sufficient assets and income.

There are basically three ways you can get a residence permit: by establishing a business in Monaco, by becoming an employee of a Monaco company or by retiring there.

For most wealthy immigrants this last category is the most relevant one, as it applies to anyone who is not going to be involved in a trading or business activity.

If you are an EU resident, to obtain a residence permit (carte de séjour) you have to apply to the Foreign Residents Section of Monaco's Sûreté Publique. You'll need to show evidence of accommodation (for example, a lease or title deeds to a property) and proof of your financial standing (for example, a bank reference).

Applications take one to two months. If you're successful you'll get a residence permit, which is initially valid for 12 months.

If you're not an EU resident, the process is only slightly more complex as you'll first need to get a visa, which more or less involves the same requirements as getting a residence permit.

While there is no personal income tax in Monaco (except for French nationals in certain circumstances), companies established in Monaco have to in theory pay a business profits tax at a rate of 35%.

In practice there are, however, a number of exceptions to the business profits tax, including:

- Businesses that are not involved in holding intellectual property or in certain trading activities (this would exempt telecommuters).
- Businesses that are involved in trading activities 75% or more of whose income comes from within Monaco, and
- Non-resident businesses conducting any business

If you set up a business and employ staff in Monaco there will be national insurance to pay which is relatively high with the employer paying up to 40%.

There are no withholding taxes in the principality.

Monaco does permit the use of trusts, however these can only be established by Monaco residents.

Overall, Monaco is an excellent choice for very wealthy expats who want to live in the heart of Europe and pay no tax (although some may regard the lifestyle as a bit 'Footballers' Wives').

PANAMA

Located in Central America, close to Costa Rica, Panama is one of the most popular and established tax havens around. Its popularity is thanks not just to the offshore companies and foundations on offer but also because those 'in the know' regard it as a good place to live.

Panama's tax advantages stem from the fact that it has a territorial tax system, just like Costa Rica, Hong Kong and Singapore. This means there is no tax on income earned outside Panama.

In fact you'll find that quite a few of the Central and South American countries won't tax any of your overseas income or gains. This makes countries such as Costa Rica, Panama, Uruguay, Nicaragua, Paraguay, Guatemala and Bolivia tax efficient for anyone who is not earning any locally derived income.

Unfortunately not all of them apply this territorial basis and, for example, Brazil, Peru, Ecuador, Chile, Mexico, Colombia and Venezuela could still tax you in full on your worldwide earnings, so you need to be careful.

This rule applies to both personal and corporate income. So income tax is only payable on income from a business carried on within Panama.

If you realize any capital gains, these are counted as income so if you have any overseas capital gains these should also be completely tax free.

If you do carry on a trade in Panama you're looking at paying income tax at a rate of 30%.

Aside from the tax benefits, Panama is popular due to its low cost of living. You'll realize by now that some of the offshore tax havens are extremely expensive places to live. Monaco and Bermuda, for example, have ridiculously high property prices.

In Panama you can buy a beautiful beachfront house (three bedrooms) for between $120,000 and $200,000.

The cost of living is about one quarter what it is in the USA ands it's a very safe place to live (the world-famous Pinkerton's

Detective Agency lists Panama as the safest place to live in all of the Americas).

Although the climate is tropical, Panama lies outside the hurricane belt.

The tax year is the same as the calendar year, ending on December 31.

In terms of tax residence, Panama applies the general rule and classes you as resident if you spend more than 180 days in any calendar year in the country.

There are special programmes to tempt foreigners to move to the country under the 'pensionado' provisions. You'll qualify provided you have a pension income of just $500 per month ($600 for a couple) which is from a government agency or a defined-benefit pension from a private company.

You'll then be entitled to Panamanian residency and a passport. You'll also be entitled to numerous discounts such as cheaper travel, discounts on meals in certain restaurants and lower hospital fees.

If you're thinking about retiring in Panama, you can also obtain residency by making a large deposit with the National Bank of Panama. This would typically last for five years and you'd need to invest enough cash for the monthly interest generated to be at least $750 (usually around $200,000). Although your capital is tied up you can withdraw interest at any time.

Therefore actually establishing overseas residence in Panama is relatively straightforward, given the programmes that are in place for both retirees and investors.

As you'd expect, Panama has no double tax treaties.

In terms of asset protection, it's also useful to look at whether there are any legal assistance treaties with other countries. For example, Belize and Costa Rica have both signed mutual legal assistance treaties with the US Government. These allow the sharing of information in criminal investigations. However, Panama hasn't signed up to any of these treaties, and so would not turn your financial records over to the US Government. It should be noted though that the mutual legal assistance treaties usually exclude pure tax offences from their scope in any case.

Panama is popular as a corporate tax haven for a number of reasons.

Its International Business Company (IBC) and foundation structures are often promoted by offshore incorporators as effective tax-avoidance tools (although, and I can't reiterate this enough, you should pay little attention to most of these advisers and get detailed advice on your *home country's* anti avoidance and other offshore legislation).

Panama also offers good value for money and, whilst not being the cheapest location for offshore company formation, is certainly significantly cheaper than the more expensive jurisdictions such as Bermuda. For example, you can set up an IBC for less than $1,500, whereas in Bermuda an offshore company could cost you four times as much.

Panama is also known for its strong maritime business and good privacy laws. Political stability is also recognized as good.

As banking and shipping are Panama's two main 'offshore' industries there is a good selection of banks to choose from (more than 140). Panamanian bank accounts are becoming more popular because interest is tax free and, for EU nationals, they are excluded from the Savings Tax Directive.

Companies are subject to the territorial tax rule, just as individuals. Therefore provided a company doesn't derive its income from Panamanian activities, there will be no tax payable.

This means that as a location for offshore IBCs Panama offers a sound 0% tax regime in most cases. This allied to the significant privacy benefits makes it a very popular destination.

ST KITTS AND NEVIS

St Kitts and Nevis is a federation of two tiny volcanic islands in the eastern Caribbean with a population of just 40,000.

The islands were discovered by Columbus in 1493 and settled by the British in the 17th century, finally becoming independent in 1983.

The climate is tropical but with a steady cool breeze for most of the year.

Crime is low and tends to be restricted to purse snatching and other petty offences.

The islands are a popular tourist destination thanks to an abundance of pristine beaches. However, if you're looking for a place in which to settle you would have to get used to the isolation.

There are very few shops and you would probably have to go to nearby St Martin to buy any luxury goods. St Kitts and Nevis levy import duties and the overall cost of living is high. Importing a car for example will set you back over 50% in import duties.

The islands have good transport links with flights to the UK and US as well as other key destinations. The main language is English.

As for tax, St Kitts and Nevis is one of the 'no-tax' havens and is becoming increasingly popular for personal offshore tax planning. The islands offer good privacy protection (which is one of the reasons St Kitts is popular in asset protection strategies) and it doesn't cost very much to set up an offshore company there.

There is no personal income tax although domestic companies face a corporation tax rate of 35%. Although this is an extremely high tax rate there is specific legislation that exempts offshore companies, as long as they only do business with non-residents.

If you work on the islands you also have to pay social security but the rates are very low – just 5% of your monthly earnings up to an earnings ceiling of $2,500 per month.

There is no capital gains tax on St Kitts and Nevis except when you sell local assets which you've owned for less than 12 months.

The fact that the islands are not a crown dependency may also be beneficial as it means they are not subject to the EU Savings Tax Directive.

This gives St Kitts an advantage over other UK dependencies in the Caribbean and over traditional UK offshore centres such as the Channel Islands.

If you want to invest in property you will have to obtain an Alien Land Holding Licence. There's also stamp duty to pay and your total purchase costs could add an extra 10% to the price.

Once a year the rental value of your property is assessed and a 5% land tax has to be paid on this rental value, although it's unlikely you would ever end up paying more than $1,000.

The good news is all your rental income is tax free and there is no capital gains tax unless you sell your property within one year.

Property is less expensive than many other islands in the Caribbean. For approximately $400,000 you can buy a decent sized villa with a swimming pool.

Prime locations with stunning ocean views will cost you a further $200,000 but you could easily end up paying over $1 million for the very best properties.

If you want to obtain a residence permit you have to complete an application form which asks for some personal details and how you intend to support yourself while living on the islands. You also have to submit evidence of your assets and a variety of other documents.

For more information go to www.stkittsnevis.org/visainfo.html.

Another reason St Kitts and Nevis are so popular is that they effectively allow you to buy citizenship and a passport.

There are a number of conditions which have to be satisfied (for example, they'll want proof that you don't have a criminal record).

The most important requirement is that you invest at least $250,000 in an 'approved investment project', which includes certain properties.

The Government also requires a registration fee ($35,000 for the main applicant, and a further $15,000 for your spouse and each child under 18).

For more information visit: www.stkittsnevis.org/citizen.html

If you want to establish permanent residence overseas quickly and perhaps even lose your UK domicile status, obtaining citizenship in St Kitts and Nevis may be useful.

SWITZERLAND

Swiss banks are the most famous in the world and have an excellent reputation for confidentiality.

As with many European countries, Switzerland taxes its residents on their worldwide income and the tax rates (which vary according to which district or 'canton' you live in can be as high as 30%.

This is not very attractive compared with other tax havens but Switzerland is not really a tax haven in the conventional sense of the word.

Foreign individuals can drastically reduce their tax bills by taking advantage of what's known as the 'Fiscal Deal'. Essentially this is a tax deal which also comes with a residence permit.

The Swiss authorities are very picky about who can take advantage of this tax saving opportunity – you'll only be able to take advantage of these tax breaks if you are prepared to become a resident, don't intend working or running a business from Switzerland and aren't a Swiss national.

You'll need to discuss the details with the particular canton in which you want to live and they'll tell you how your taxable income will be calculated.

A common assessment could be that your taxable income might be deemed to be a multiple of what you pay for property rental.

In order to apply for the Fiscal Deal you'll need to be worth not less than two million Swiss Francs (roughly £880,000, or $1.5 million).

Just like with the Gibraltar HNWI scheme the tax rates payable under this system are the same as would apply normally – it's just that the amount of taxable income is restricted to a much lower level.

The drawback (aside from the minimum net wealth requirement) is that you would not be able to work or run a business in Switzerland. Fine if you're independently wealthy but not so great if you still have to earn a living.

The Fiscal Deal is a famous part of the Swiss tax system and has been used by many famous people to avoid tax.

The qualifying income requirements will depend on the particular Canton, however as a guide you'd probably need to have taxable income of at least $60,000 a year to be eligible.

In addition to the income taxes the Swiss have:

- Capital gains tax on property disposals averaging 18%.
- Social security which can be pretty high if you are an employee (roughly 13%), although this doesn't affect residents under the Fiscal Deal as they're not allowed to gain employment in any case.
- Inheritance tax is levied by some of the Cantons, so if you want to avoid or minimize IHT you need to be flexible as to where you live (for example, the canton of Schwyz does not charge any inheritance tax and many of the others don't charge inheritance tax on transfers to spouses and children).
- A wealth tax, again levied by the cantons, which is payable by residents on the value of all assets in Switzerland (often at a rate of 1.5%).

Tax issues aside, Switzerland offers an enviable lifestyle in the heart of Europe. The property prices, whilst certainly not low, are reasonable and far cheaper than many parts of London. Crime is low and the climate is mild in many parts of the country.

However, you must be prepared to pay for the privilege of being a Swiss resident as the cost of living is high (amongst the highest in Europe, along with Norway and Iceland).

In terms of corporate tax, a company is deemed to be resident in Switzerland if it is either incorporated in Switzerland or effectively managed from there (a similar rule to the UK).

Resident companies have to pay tax on their worldwide income, however, non-resident companies only pay tax on profits generated from property and permanent establishments located in Switzerland.

As you'd expect the Swiss take banking secrecy very seriously and although Switzerland does exchange information with other tax authorities, this will only be done when there is a case of serious tax fraud.

In addition, the Swiss authorities will only exchange information where the offence is also an offence in Switzerland.

Given that they have a pretty narrow view of tax fraud, as a matter of practice this will reduce the instances of information exchange.

If you're looking at having one of the famous Swiss bank accounts, you should read Chapter 9 on the impact of the European Savings Tax Directive.

TURKS & CAICOS ISLANDS

The Turks and Caicos are made up of 45 islands and cays located south-east of the Bahamas. The total population is less than 20,000, most of whom live on Providenciales (Provo), the biggest of the islands.

The Turks and Caicos are a British overseas territory (much like many of the other Caribbean tax havens) and enjoy self-rule under a Governor and elected council.

As you'd expect, the official language is English and the legal system is derived largely from English law. The economy is dependent on financial services and tourism (miles of coral reefs and white beaches).

Crime is very low and the infrastructure is generally good with broadband internet access and a good but expensive telephone service.

There are direct flights to the US and Canada.

The Turks and Caicos offer the same tax benefits as many of the other Caribbean tax havens. There is no:

- Income tax
- Capital gains tax
- Inheritance tax

The Government raises money through indirect taxes such as import duties and stamp duty (which ranges from 0% to almost 10%).

The Turks and Caicos have strict banking confidentiality laws and the unauthorized disclosure of confidential information is a crime.

While there is a treaty in place with the US allowing for the exchange of information relating to serious criminal offences, tax matters are specifically excluded from the ambit of the treaty.

Note that as a UK crown dependency the Turks and Caicos will be implementing the EU Savings Tax Directive and implementing a withholding tax for EU residents.

This may make it a less attractive tax haven than other countries in the region such as Panama, Antigua and the Bahamas, all of which are not bound by the provisions of the directive.

Property prices vary enormously. You can pick up small plots for under $50,000 or a large beachfront plot for over $2 million. I've seen entry-level apartments for $260,000 and top-of-the-range condos going for over $6 million.

A two-bedroom house with shared pool could be yours for around $330,000.

If you buy property as an investment, all your returns will, of course, be tax free.

Because of the necessity to import practically everything, the cost of living on the islands is comparatively high.

If you're looking to emigrate there permanently you could consider obtaining a Permanent Residence Certificate. In order to obtain one you would need to make an investment in local property or a local business.

The minimum investment required is $250,000 on Providenciales and $125,000 on the other islands.

If you want to work on the Turks and Caicos islands you need to obtain a work permit. As with other Caribbean countries they are careful to preserve jobs for locals, so you need to have special skills.

There are a number of different corporate entities you can set up including an International Business Company (IBC), limited partnership, hybrid company or trust.

As you'd expect there is no tax levied on any of these. In fact when you form an IBC you'll automatically receive a certificate of tax exemption for a period of 20 years. This is a guarantee that the authorities won't change their minds and implement a corporate tax on income or gains during the 20-year period.

Therefore the Turks and Caicos, along with other Caribbean jurisdictions offer a tax-free lifestyle and straightforward residency requirements both for individuals and companies.

UNITED STATES

Certainly not a traditional tax haven by any stretch of the imagination, the US does offer some specific tax-saving opportunities.

In particular a US limited liability company (LLC) is often a useful tool in international tax planning.

This is because LLCs that carry on no business in the US and derive no income from any sources within the US do not need to file a US federal tax return.

An LLC is a cross between a partnership and a company. It provides the benefit of limited liability that a company offers, but also gives the 'pass through taxation' benefits of a partnership (the profits are taxed in the hands of the partners instead of in the company).

In other words, the tax status of the LLC would depend on the residence of its members. Non-US individuals trading outside the US via an LLC would therefore not be liable to pay US tax on the LLCs profits.

The US can therefore be a useful intermediary for foreign business and investments. In particular, one of the benefits is access to the USA's wide tax treaty network.

We'll take a closer look at the uses to which offshore companies can be put in Chapter 6. However a good use for a US LLC may be as part of a re-invoicing strategy. This involves interposing an LLC between a trader and a customer and, in effect, diverting a proportion of the profit to the LLC. The payments would be made in exchange for the LLC providing services to the trading company (for example, administrative services).

LLCs can be set up in many of the US states, however the favoured states are Delaware or Nevada as these offer the best tax options as well as minimal administrative requirements.

If you did set up a US LLC this would not need to file a US tax return or pay US income tax provided any trade in question is carried on outside the US.

DENMARK

Although Denmark is generally accepted as being one of the most expensive and overtaxed countries in the world, it does offer a number of tax-saving benefits to the astute non-resident.

The most popular strategy is setting up a zero-tax holding company. Some of the big international conglomerates such as Pepsico do this.

There are a few conditions that need to be satisfied to obtain this zero-tax status but these are not difficult to satisfy and the benefits more than outweigh the inconvenience of jumping through a few hoops.

The advantage of using Denmark is that it has a substantial number of double tax treaties with other countries. This makes it an ideal place to establish a holding company as this allows dividends to be transferred from subsidiaries based in various parts of the world without any tax being deducted. See Chapter 7 on holding companies for more details of the advantages of Danish holding companies.

UNITED KINGDOM

Again, not your traditional tax haven but the UK has some very useful tax laws which can be exploited by astute individuals.

In particular the domicile rules allow foreign persons to live in the UK and pay no tax on their overseas income and capital gains, provided these amounts are not remitted to the UK.

In terms of business entities the UK has introduced a relatively new type of business structure known as the Limited Liability Partnership (LLP). If certain circumstances are met, the LLP can effectively operate free of any UK tax.

For all intents and purposes, the British LLP is comparable to a United States LLC: it is a combination of a standard limited liability company and a partnership.

Just like limited companies, LLPs provide limited liability to members (in contrast to partnerships where partners' liability is unlimited). However, LLPs are still treated as partnerships as far as taxation is concerned and tax is assessed individually on each member after the distribution of the LLP's profits among them. The LLP as such is not taxed at all.

The legislation requires that an LLP has at least two members. They may be of any nationality and need not be UK residents. (It's worth noting that the US LLC can have only one member.)

In fact, provided the LLP members are located outside the United Kingdom and no business is conducted with or within the UK, the LLP has no liability for UK taxation.

For a UK non-resident an LLP is an excellent addition to a collection of 'non-offshore' yet tax-free corporate entities.

LABUAN

Labuan is a small East Malaysian island in the South China Sea. In 1990 the Malaysian Government set it up as an International Offshore Financial Centre.

It's fair to say that Labuan has remained a fairly low-key tax haven, attractive for those wishing to keep out of the spotlight.

Offshore Trading Companies in Labuan pay 3% tax on profits or a fixed sum of RM20,000 (around $5,000), whichever is lower. If you form an investment or non-trading company you won't pay any tax at all.

If privacy is important the company can simply elect to pay the maximum tax of RM20,000 per annum and there would then be no need to file accounts.

There is also no capital gains tax in Labuan.

In addition to this, Labuan does not impose any disclosure requirements as regards beneficial ownership. So all in all it offers some attractive tax-saving opportunities, depending on your own personal residence position, plus some attractive privacy protection benefits.

FLOATING TAX HAVENS

If you like travelling and are fond of the sea you could consider living on a boat. You would need to be careful about where you locate it as it wouldn't be possible to simply moor offshore and claim non-residence status.

Most developed countries also tax individuals living on boats within their territorial waters. The UK, for example, taxes individuals within 12 nautical miles of the shore.

Alternatively, if you have a few million to spare and are a member of the super-rich you could buy an apartment on *The World*, which is a newly launched luxury cruise ship.

Getting yourself an apartment on this luxury super ship doesn't come cheap. About 110 permanent apartments with between one and three bedrooms were for sale on the ship with prices starting at £1.6 million and rising to over £5 million.

This amount of money buys you a luxurious fully fitted apartment (with internet access, of course, so you can telecommute while cruising around the globe!)

The key benefit of The World is that the boat sails around the world all year round so people who live on board can be true 'nautical nomads' and escape being classed as tax resident in any particular country (although US citizens would need to be careful, as a tax charge could apply even if non-resident).

Whilst this is certainly beneficial you should note that if you are conducting a trade in a particular country, you could still have to pay tax in the country where the business is based unless, of course, you are trading out of a tax haven. Furthermore, you would not be able to make use of any double tax treaties (as you wouldn't be officially resident anywhere!)

If you want to go one up from a boat you could consider joining one of the 'offshore communities' being proposed. The plan here is to create an entire town in the middle of the sea (on a mobile platform). There will be houses, shops, cinemas, recreation facilities, restaurants and so on and the platform will travel the entire globe always remaining in international waters.

Whether many people could live so cut off from the rest of the world is debatable. However, it would be the ultimate tax haven with no taxes at all. One point to bear in mind is that you'd also need to carefully consider whether your home country would accept that you are non-resident if you cannot prove that you are resident in another country.

Another alternative is to purchase your own yacht.

When most people think of yachts they think of the impressive boats you find moored in jet set locations such as Monaco. However, if sailing is your thing, you could probably purchase a large yacht capable of comfortable and safe ocean travel for under $200,000.

It would be kitted out like a home from home and most would offer air-conditioning and all the latest mod cons.

Again you would need to travel pretty regularly in order to avoid being classed as resident in any jurisdiction, however this may not be that difficult in practice.

It's likely that the number of 'nautical nomads' will continue to grow in places where countries are close and welcome visitors. The Caribbean is a perfect example as some of the islands are within 25 miles of each other and many permit visitors to stay for three months at a time on tourists visas.

What's more, many of the Caribbean countries have no taxes so even if you do stay for too long in any one jurisdiction the tax implications may not be significant.

Chapter 3

Living in a Tax Haven

Possibly the easiest way to escape tax in one country is to move to another!

With more and more people 'telecommuting' (working from remote mobile offices), doing your job or running your business in another country may not prove such a problem.

While most countries, such as the UK, tax the worldwide income of their residents, they do not tax citizens who leave the country and become non-resident.

So a UK a citizen can escape high UK tax bills simply by moving to a low-tax country.

Most countries treat you as non-resident if you are absent for six to nine months.

However this is not always the case. Certain countries such as the US, Finland and the Philippines tax their *citizens*, no matter where they live.

So if you're a US citizen and go and live in the Bahamas for 10 years you'll still have to pay US tax on all your income (subject to a limited exemption for overseas earned income).

To escape the US tax net completely you would have to relinquish your citizenship and acquire another one.

Citizens of most other countries, such as the UK, can escape the taxman's clutches by becoming non-resident.

However, certain countries make it more difficult than others to lose your resident status.

For example, in Sweden you are regarded as resident if:

• Your 'real home and dwelling' is in Sweden, or

- Your 'habitual abode' is in Sweden, or

- You previously had a 'real home and dwelling' there and you have an 'essential connection' with Sweden.

'Essential connection' means, for instance, that you had Swedish property or family in Sweden.

Another big stumbling block is that anyone who has spent more then 10 years in Sweden is deemed to remain resident for five years after leaving, unless they can prove that they have no 'essential connection' with the country.

Similar rules apply in Holland. The factors that determine your residence status include the number of days you spend in Holland during the tax year, whether you own Dutch property and whether you have any family there.

This shows how easy it is to come within the scope of two countries' tax regimes. A Swedish person emigrating to the US could easily be classed as both Swedish resident, as well as US resident (if they actually live in the US). In this case, though, the US-Sweden tax treaty would come into play to decide in which of the two countries the individual is resident.

The Dutch sometimes also levy an 'exit' tax on residents and inheritance tax applies for up to 10 years after your residence has ceased. So avoiding Dutch tax is a long-term process.

Other countries also have an 'emigration tax'.

For example, let's say you have UK investment property and become Australian resident. When you eventually sell the property you will only pay Australian capital gains tax on profits made *after* entering the country. All your profits made prior to becoming an Australian resident will be tax free.

In tax speak we say there is an 'uplift' in the asset's base cost: the cost of the asset is no longer what you paid for it but is deemed to be its market value when you entered the country. A higher cost means less profit and therefore less tax.

The drawback is that if you cease to be Australian resident your investments are deemed to have been sold (even if they haven't) which means that emigrants can end up with hefty capital gains tax bills when they leave the country.

There is fortunately a concession (known as the '5-in-10' concession) which exempts assets held by anyone who has lived in Australia for less than five out of the previous 10 years. As a result many expat workers are not trapped by this piece of tax law.

In summary, moving overseas can be an effective way to drastically cut your tax bill. Some countries like the UK will largely stop taxing you when you leave while others, like the US, will tax you wherever you go.

The Source Basis vs The Residence Basis

It's also important to distinguish between the 'source' basis of taxation and the 'residence' basis. Most countries use one or the other.

Under the source basis it doesn't matter what your residence status is: your income is taxed if it arises within the country's borders. So if you are a resident of Atlantis and emigrate to Narnia, you will still have to pay tax in Atlantis on the investments you left behind.

By contrast, under the residence basis, Atlantis will stop taxing you once you become non-resident.

A lot of countries tax income that arises within their borders by default. For example, tax is deducted in the UK from interest earned by non-residents. However, someone who is not 'ordinarily' resident in the UK can apply to have interest paid gross (without tax deducted).

You have to be careful if you plan to move to a tax haven and continue running a business in your home country. Most countries tax trading income arising within their boundaries.

There are, however, two exceptions to this rule:

- If you go and live in a country that has a double tax treaty with the country where your business is based. In this case you will probably only pay local tax on profits arising from a permanent establishment (in other words, a business with a physical presence in the country, such as offices).

> The problem is finding a country that has a good double tax treaty network AND a low domestic tax regime. This is why Cyprus and Ireland are popular tax havens.

- If your business is based in a genuine 'no tax' haven. There would then be no local taxes on your trading profits.

Becoming a UK Non-resident

There is no formal legal definition of 'residence'. The UK Inland Revenue's practice – based on a mixture of statute and court decisions – is to regard you as resident in the UK during a tax year if:

- You spend 183 days or more in the UK during the tax year, or

- Although here for less than 183 days, you have spent more than 90 days per year in the country over the past four years (taken as an average). You will then be classed as UK resident from the fifth year.

These rules have no statutory force and are guidance only. For example, an individual who regularly returns to the UK for 87 days per tax year may still be regarded as UK resident.

A person can also be resident in two countries at the same time. It is therefore not possible to escape UK residence by arguing that you are resident elsewhere.

It is important to note that UK residence is a question of fact and not intention. Therefore although you may intend to leave before the 183-day limit, if you are forced to remain in the UK as a result of exceptional circumstances you will nevertheless be regarded as UK resident.

Even if you qualify as non-resident you may still fall into the taxman's clutches by being classified as *UK ordinarily resident*.

There is also no statutory test of ordinary residence. You will be classified as a UK ordinary resident if the UK is your 'normal place of residence'.

On leaving the country you will continue to be regarded as ordinarily resident unless you go abroad with the intention of taking up permanent residence overseas.

The Inland Revenue normally interprets 'permanent' to mean three years or more.

It is therefore possible to be non-UK resident but UK ordinarily resident. This would occur, for example, where you go abroad for a long holiday and do not return to the UK during a particular tax year. You will continue to be classed as UK ordinarily resident until you can show that you have taken up a permanent residence elsewhere.

The consequence of being classed as UK ordinarily resident is that you will still have to pay UK capital gains tax on your worldwide capital gains.

A person who is UK resident under the 183-day test may not necessarily be UK ordinarily resident. Such a person would then have to pay tax on overseas income and gains that are brought into the UK (this applies for Commonwealth and Irish citizens).

However, a person who is UK resident as a result of the 90-day test would find it difficult to argue that he or she is not also UK ordinarily resident and therefore worldwide income and gains would be taxed as they arise, not just when brought into the UK.

One factor that is likely to be taken into account in assessing ordinary residence is whether you continue to own and occupy property in the UK – in particular, where the use or occupation of the property is combined with other factors, such as regular visits to the UK only slightly below the 90-day average. This will be persuasive evidence that you have not taken up a permanent residence elsewhere.

However, subject to this, a person who leaves the UK will cease to be UK ordinarily resident if he or she establishes non-UK residence for three consecutive tax years.

Capital Gains Tax Planning

One of the main reasons people use tax havens is to escape capital gains tax (CGT).

Individuals with large property or share portfolios or a business to sell often consider moving overseas to a country with low or no capital gains tax.

To do this successfully UK residents must ensure they are not UK resident or UK ordinarily resident.

The good news is that if CGT avoidance is your top priority there are a lot of countries that don't tax capital gains.

Cyprus is a popular choice for UK expats because it allows you to avoid CGT on UK land and property disposals and also offers advantageous income tax treatment of pensions.

The Importance of Timing

Timing is crucial in offshore tax planning and should be built into your 'escape plan' from early on.

For example, there's no point moving to a tax haven to sell your investment properties if you still end up paying tax in the country you leave.

This could easily happen if you don't understand your home country's capital gains tax rules for emigrants.

For example, it could be the case that you can become non-resident half way through a tax year for *income tax* purposes. But for *capital gains tax* purposes you may need to be a non-resident for the *entire* tax year.

If you leave the UK and sell assets later in the *same tax year*, you will still have to pay UK capital gains tax.

To avoid capital gains tax you have to sell your assets in the *next tax year*.

You'll also find similar rules in the US, as well as many other European countries.

Another way you may get caught out is by selling assets en route to another high-tax country. For example, if you emigrate from the UK to Country X and decide to stop off in the Cayman Islands to dispose of your UK properties, any gain could still be subject to tax in Country X if you're classed as resident for the entire tax year.

Therefore as a general rule you are much safer if you conduct all your dealings in *separate tax years*:

- Dispose of assets in a separate tax year from the year you emigrate.

- Dispose of assets, if possible, in a separate tax year from the year you acquire residence in your new home country.

Clearly it is crucial to understand how different countries apply the definition of residence.

If you can find a country that allows 'split-year' residence you may have nothing to fear. The split-year basis means that you will only pay tax on income or gains that arise *after* you become a resident in that country.

So if you sell assets early in the tax year and then become resident in another country a few months later, you will not be subject to tax.

The UK applies such a split-year rule in certain circumstances, as does the US.

You become a US resident for tax purposes as soon as you become a permanent resident. You will then have to declare your worldwide income to the IRS.

Of course lots of immigrants find themselves becoming US resident during a tax year, with part of the tax year having been spent in another country such as the UK.

This is known as a 'dual status' tax year. As a dual-status taxpayer you will be taxed on income and capital gains from all sources for the part of the year you are a US resident.

You will also be taxed on income and gains derived in the US for the *entire tax year*. Income from a trade or business conducted in the United States will also be taxed.

Note that income and gains you receive from sources outside the US before you become resident is usually not taxable. Therefore if you acquire US residence via a green card you can usually escape US tax by selling any overseas assets prior to actually becoming US resident.

Some people become 'tax nomads' ensuring they are not resident in any country. This is difficult to achieve long term but ideal for a couple of years to shield large capital gains or one-off income payments.

However, if you keep hold of income-producing assets in your home country your options are more limited. UK rental income and trading income, for example, is usually taxed even if you become non-resident.

Most tax treaties between countries state that the country where the property is physically located can tax the rental income. In the UK the Non-resident Landlord Scheme requires letting agent or tenants to withhold tax from the rent paid to an overseas landlord.

In these cases the main focus is on maximizing your tax deductions. Ways you could do this include moving offshore and forming an offshore personal service company that invoices your UK trading company. These amounts would be tax deductible and reduce your taxable profits in the UK. At the same time the payments from the UK company could be received tax free.

As for rental income, obtaining offshore loans and claiming the interest as a tax deduction is a popular technique.

Chapter 4

How Offshore Trusts Can Help You

What is a Trust?

Offshore trusts are set up for lots of different reasons. The most popular are tax avoidance and privacy protection. For example, offshore trusts are often used in conjunction with offshore companies. By making a trust a shareholder of the company the beneficial ownership of the company can stay completely confidential.

The beauty of a trust is that it lets you transfer ownership of your assets while still having a say as to how they are used. So rather than give a large cash amount to your teenage son, you could establish a trust for his benefit, and transfer the cash to the trust. As well as having important family financial planning benefits, they can also have tax and asset protection advantages.

The basic idea is that if the assets are no longer yours you don't have to pay tax. And if the assets aren't legally yours, creditors and others won't be able to get their hands on them either.

There are various people involved in setting up and running a trust:

- **Trustees**. These are the people who actually run the trust and decide how the trust's assets are used (subject to the trust agreement). There are usually at least two trustees and, as their name implies, it's essential that they are people you can trust.

  In some cases a professional trustee may be used. This could be either a solicitor, accountant or a firm that specializes in trust administration. There are lots of specialist trust firms based in the various tax havens.

- **Beneficiaries**. These are the individuals who actually benefit from the trust's assets. They could, for example, be allowed to use a property owned by the trust or receive income from the trust's investments.

Beneficiaries can have different types of interest in the assets. For example, a life interest could allow a property to be used during a beneficiary's lifetime. A residual interest would then give someone else the right to benefit after the life interest beneficiary has died.

- **Settlor**. The settlor is the individual who gifts the assets to the trust in the first place. Unless the settlor is also a trustee he will have no automatic influence over how the assets are used, although as a matter of course the trustees would be guided by the settlor, especially if he has chosen them well.

Apart from choosing the trustees carefully, there are two key ways that a settlor can provide guidance as to how the trust assets are used:

- First, the settlor can draft a letter of wishes. The content of the letter will be entirely up to the particular settlor. It could be a general letter covering his aims in setting up the trust and what he hopes to achieve or it could be a highly specific letter listing allowable and non allowable payments from the trust.

  Typically, the letter of wishes will show the trustees what the settlor's purpose was in setting up the trust, the type of investments the trust should make and the type of payouts the trustees should consider. Although not binding, the letter of wishes would usually be taken seriously by the trustees.

- Second, and perhaps most important, is the trust agreement. This is the document that actually establishes the trust and will provide the scope of the trustees powers. The settlor should ensure that any particular requirements regarding the trust are set out clearly in this document.

  One of the most important functions of the trust agreement is defining when and under what circumstances the beneficiaries will be entitled to benefit from the trust.

There is therefore a high degree of flexibility and the trust could lay out various conditions that have to be met before benefits can be enjoyed.

Typical conditions could be:

- Preventing minors from benefiting until they reach a certain age, for example 18 or 21.

- Stopping trust benefits once beneficiaries exceed a certain age, for example 30.

- Providing benefits to future grandchildren.

- Ceasing benefits if beneficiaries become non-resident.

- Granting benefits as reward for specific achievements such as obtaining a university degree or other qualification.

- Stopping trust benefits when a beneficiary becomes married or remarries.

Tax Benefits of Trusts

Trusts can be used for a variety of tax-saving purposes. One of the most popular is emigration tax planning.

Someone who has decided to emigrate could transfer a substantial part of their assets to an offshore trust before taking up residence in the new country. The idea here is to prevent the new country taxing the immigrant's income and assets.

Two common jurisdictions where immigrant trusts are used are Canada and the UK.

Canada and the Immigrant Trust

A Canadian resident is subject to Canadian income tax on his or her worldwide income from the date Canadian residence is obtained.

Canada operates a split-year system which means that when you become resident, the tax year is split into the non-resident part and the resident part.

In the non-resident period, only *Canadian* income is taxed. When you become resident your worldwide income is taxed.

If you own property or shares you will only pay tax on capital gains that arise *after* you obtain Canadian residence. This is a useful tax break for people who are already sitting on large capital gains.

However, new immigrants can also shelter their foreign income and capital gains for a further five years after becoming Canadian resident by transferring assets into an offshore trust in a tax haven such as the Bahamas.

Any amounts paid to a beneficiary who is a Canadian resident (for example, your children) will be taxable but it is usually possible to structure these payments as capital distributions so they escape Canadian tax.

In order for this setup to be effective the trust must be established before you become Canadian resident.

After the five years are up you'll start paying Canadian tax on the trust's assets so at this point you may wish to wind up the trust.

It's important, therefore, to weigh up the tax savings with the cost of setting up and dismantling the trust.

UK Immigrants

Trusts are also used by those who emigrate to the UK. Assets could be transferred into an offshore trust prior to obtaining UK residence. The assets of the offshore trust would then not be part of the immigrant's estate for inheritance tax purposes.

Similar principles apply in other countries and if your intention is to own assets in a high-tax country, using an offshore trust will often take the assets out of the scope of certain domestic taxes.

Inheritance taxes, in particular, can be avoided by setting up offshore trusts.

UK Residents and Trusts

There are a number of provisions designed to prevent people who already live in the UK setting up an offshore trust and escaping the taxman's clutches.

These 'trust-busting' rules are highly complex but the basic gist in that they can be used to force the person who sets up the trust or the beneficiaries to pay tax on the trust's income and capital gains.

Anyone wanting to set up a trust should always take professional advice to find out whether these trust-busting rules will apply.

The following are some of the situations where an offshore trust could still be used effectively by a UK resident:

Where the *Settlor* is Not UK Domiciled

People who are not UK domiciled are in a privileged position as they can potentially use trusts to avoid certain UK taxes.

For example, a non-domiciled person could establish a trust to hold overseas property. If the trust is classed as an 'excluded property trust' the assets would fall out of the UK inheritance tax net.

Those who intend to live in the UK for the long term (but are not UK domiciled) could use this arrangement to protect their overseas assets in the event that they become UK domiciled (you can be deemed UK domiciled for inheritance tax purposes after having been resident for 17 years).

Where the *Beneficiaries* are Not UK Domiciled

Anti-avoidance rules tax capital gains in the hands of a trust's beneficiaries in certain circumstances. However, if the beneficiaries are non-UK domiciled (or non-UK resident) these rules do not apply. An offshore trust could therefore realize gains and make overseas payments to UK resident but non-domiciled individuals free of tax.

Where no family members are beneficiaries

These are difficult to achieve in practice but could be made by remote relations or friends. These offshore trusts would act as a shelter from UK tax on both income and capital gains. This means that any gains or overseas income the trust generates would not be taxed in the hands of the settlor.

Where the Trust is Designed for Income Tax Avoidance and the Beneficiaries are Children and Grandchildren

The capital gains tax anti-avoidance provisions are much stricter than the income tax provisions. Therefore while an offshore trust formed with children or grandchildren being the beneficiaries would be exempt from UK income tax on overseas income and gains, the gains of the trust would be attributed to a UK-resident settlor of the trust. The overseas income would not, however, so the trust could avoid paying any UK tax on any foreign income.

Where the Trust Owns Shares in Overseas Trading Companies

There are a couple of reasons why using a trust to own shares in overseas trading companies may prove effective. Firstly, a UK resident would find it easier to argue that a company is non-UK resident if the shares in the company are owned by a non-UK resident trust.

Secondly, and linked to trusts for children and grandchildren, a common example would be for the trust to hold shares in a non-UK resident trading company (operating wholly abroad). Profits would be paid to the trust from the company, but as this represents foreign income it would not be apportioned to the UK resident taxpayer and could be held in the trust for the benefit of the children.

One of the main problems for a UK resident thinking of setting up an offshore trust is that any capital gains from property, shares and other assets could be taxed if the settlor or his family can benefit from the trust.

Similarly, income of the trust could be taxed if the settlor or his spouse can benefit.

Therefore simply setting up a trust to hold overseas assets for the benefit of a settlor and his spouse is unlikely to yield any UK tax advantages.

As for inheritance tax, establishing a trust can be beneficial as it can take the assets out of the estate of the transferor. However, in the UK most trusts are subject to a separate inheritance tax regime, so avoiding inheritance tax by using trusts is certainly not straightforward, although it's fair to say that they can be used to reduce tax.

Offshore Companies Owned by a Trust

Offshore trusts are often used together with offshore companies for enhanced confidentiality.

There are different types of trusts, however you would usually use a discretionary trust for this type of arrangement. With a discretionary trust the trustees are able to use their 'discretion' as to who benefits and by how much.

Often such trusts are formed to guarantee privacy over your assets. You may not need to be a named beneficiary of this type of trust – or named in any other way.

To make this work, the trustee and the settlor would usually all be residents of a country other than your own.

The discretionary trust would then own the offshore company which itself would own various assets such as property.

The offshore company can have a nominee director and secretary or alternatively you could use bearer shares if you use an International Business Company (IBC) incorporated in a suitable jurisdiction (for example, a Cayman exempt company).

With bearer shares the person who holds the share certificates is the person who owns the company. Ownership is transferred simply by handing over the share certificates to someone else.

They're available in a number of offshore tax havens specializing in privacy protection. In many jurisdictions, using an offshore trust and company structure would allow you to legally absolve yourself of ownership of the offshore company and its assets, which would instead be owned by the trust.

For UK individuals, using the offshore trust/company structure is often beneficial as it would make it easier to argue that the company itself is not UK resident.

An offshore company could still be UK resident (and therefore subject to UK taxes on worldwide income and gains) if it is controlled and managed from the UK.

If there are UK directors and shareholders it would be difficult to argue that the company is not managed and controlled from the UK.

By using an offshore trust to hold the shares in the company, provided it is the offshore trustees that exercise control over the directors, it is easier to argue the company is controlled outside the UK and is non-resident (resulting in overseas income and capital gains being exempt from UK corporation tax).

Another common scenario is for the settlor (the person who sets up the trust) to offer services to the trust for a fee (for example, managing properties or investigating investment opportunities).

In this role, you can also claim expenses for costs you incur as well as take out a loan from the company and purchase assets for the company.

Note that you'd need to be careful to ensure that legal documentation was in place to clearly establish the relationship between you and the offshore company.

This allows you to extract cash from the trust without remaining a trust beneficiary. This can be useful because, as we've seen, many jurisdictions, such as the UK and many European countries, have anti-avoidance legislation that applies where a settlor is also a beneficiary. These rules can force the settlor to pay tax on the income of the trust. Using the independent contractor route can help to circumvent these rules.

If you're looking at establishing a trust, as stated previously, you should ensure that you have trustees that you really can trust. It's also advisable to have a trust 'protector' who can replace the trustees if necessary.

The cost of setting up an offshore trust structure will vary depending on the type of trust and whether there are any offshore companies involved. You're probably looking at less than £1,000 for a simple trust to over £10,000 for a more complex arrangement.

Where is the Best Place to Locate an Offshore Trust?

There are numerous countries that offer a good regime for setting up an offshore trust.

A trust can operate anywhere in the world. The only requirement is that the jurisdiction under which the trust is established recognizes the legal concept of the trust.

Aside from the tax implications you should consider the running of the trust and keep an eye of the costs involved (both the initial set up costs and the ongoing administration costs).

For most people the most important considerations when deciding where to set up an offshore trust are:

- Asset protection and confidentiality
- Tax savings

The countries below are all recognized as good places to set up an offshore trust:

- Jersey/Guernsey
- Liechtenstein
- St Kitts and Nevis
- Panama
- The Bahamas
- Austria
- New Zealand
- Netherlands Antilles

This list is by no means exhaustive and depending on the use of the trust and location of the beneficiaries and settlor, other countries such as Mauritius and Belize could also be considered.

In particular, significant non-tax considerations could be paramount including:

- The language used in the jurisdiction
- The time difference between you and the country in question
- The political and financial stability of the tax haven
- The geographical location – in case you need to visit in person
- The costs associated with setting up and running the trust

For example, someone wanting to trade with China might be better off setting up a trust in Mauritius as opposed to St Kitts, due to Mauritius's proximity and good relationship with China.

Chapter 5

Escaping the Taxman's Clutches

Many high-tax countries have what are known as 'controlled foreign company' (CFC) laws to prevent people making use of tax havens.

Essentially the fact that the company is located in a tax haven is ignored and the profits are all taxed in, say, the UK if the company is viewed as being controlled by someone living in the UK.

These laws are designed to stop individuals and companies shifting profits to tax havens.

The exact arrangements vary widely from country to country but countries that have CFC rules include:

- United States
- United Kingdom
- Canada
- Australia
- Spain
- France
- Germany

So if you're considering using an offshore company or trust you should always look at the CFC or other anti-avoidance rules in your country of residence and assess how they affect your tax planning.

You can then look at the options available for circumventing these rules. A common example is to ensure that you don't fall foul of the 'ownership requirement'.

Many CFC regulations impose a minimum ownership of the overseas entity before the rules will 'bite'. Provided you own less than the minimum you should be safe.

For instance, the UK has special controlled foreign company legislation that affects any overseas company that is owned by a UK company.

If the overseas company is classed as a CFC, its profits are apportioned to any UK companies who hold an interest in it, provided the percentage of the profits apportioned is at least 25%.

There are however some exemptions available to prevent the CFC rules from applying.

Before falling within the CFC rules a company would first need to meet the definition of a 'controlled foreign company'.

A CFC is defined as a *company* that is:

- Not UK resident,
- Controlled from the UK, and
- Subject to overseas tax which is less than 75% of the equivalent UK tax.

So the first point to note is that the UK CFC regime will not apply if you are an *individual* owning an overseas company. (Instead other anti-avoidance legislation could apply which we'll look at shortly.)

The CFC provisions will only apply if your overseas company is owned by a UK resident company.

There are, however, lots of exemptions to the CFC rules including:

- If the overseas company follows an acceptable distribution policy. If the CFC pays dividends of at least 90% of its profits to the UK company, the CFC profits will not fall within the CFC provisions.

- Low profits. Provided chargeable profits (excluding gains) are less than £50,000, no tax will arise under the CFC provisions.

- The motive test. Essentially if you can show that tax avoidance was not the main purpose behind setting up the company the CFC provisions will also not apply.

The US by contrast has its own CFC legislation. This defines a CFC as:

"any foreign corporation of which more than fifty percent of its value or voting stock is owned by United States shareholders on any one day during the taxable year of such Foreign Corporation".

A US shareholder is also specifically defined as a US citizen or entity (in other words, an individual or a company or trust) holding or controlling more than 10% of the shares.

Example

Let's say that the shares in Bob Ltd, a British Virgin Islands company, are held by the following people:

- Jake a US resident owns 50%
- Jason a US resident owns 11%
- Peter a resident of the Caymans owns 39%

Under the existing US tax rules, Bob Inc is a CFC because more than 50% of the voting stock is held by US shareholders.

As a result, the profits of the CFC could be apportioned directly to the shareholders and taxed in the US.

The simplest way to avoid ending up with a CFC is to ensure that less than 50% of the shares are held by US shareholders – and no individual shareholder holds more than 10% of the shares.

One way of doing this is to use a foundation or trust to hold more than 50% of the shares. However, in the US there are also passive investment rules that could apply.

The US tax authorities make a distinction between income earned from a foreign business and income generated by passive investments. Income earned by a trading business can usually stay untaxed until it is extracted by a US resident.

Investment income usually becomes caught up in the passive investment rules that result in a much more complicated and unfavourable tax treatment and can lead to unrealised profits being taxed.

Examples of How to Commonly Avoid the CFC Rules

- Set up a new business in a tax haven such as Cyprus or Gibraltar with ownership that falls outside the CFC rules (for example, for US tax purposes don't hold more than 40% from US shareholders) and put the rest of the shares in trust for children or in the hands of an offshore relative.

- Create a joint venture with other companies or individuals so that ownership is sufficiently diversified so that you escape the CFC rules and the ownership requirements.

UK Provisions for Individuals

You'll notice from this that the US provisions apply to individuals and companies, whereas the UK provisions only apply to companies. This doesn't mean that UK individuals have free rein to use offshore companies and trusts.

The UK has similar provisions that apply to individuals. One of these is S739 ICTA 1988.

This gives the taxman wide-ranging powers to prevent income tax avoidance by individuals using offshore companies and trusts.

S739 applies to an individual who transfers assets or is associated with a transfer by somebody else.

The conditions for application of Section 739 are:

- There must be a transfer of assets by an individual.
- As a result of the transfer, income becomes payable to a non-resident person.
- The transferor must have power to enjoy that income in some way or be entitled to receive a capital sum.
- The transferor must be ordinarily resident in the UK in the year in question.

If all of these conditions are fulfilled the income that becomes payable to the offshore company or trust is deemed to be that of the individual who made the transfer, to the extent that he has power to enjoy that income.

The first point to consider is whether there has been a 'transfer of assets' by you. The UK tax authorities take a wide view of what constitutes a transfer of assets.

For example, S739 may apply where an individual transfers cash to establish a non-resident trust or subscribes for the share capital of an offshore company or where an individual transfers assets such as shares or property to a new or existing non-resident company or trust in a tax haven.

It can also apply where intangible assets are transferred, for example where a UK individual transfers his services to an offshore company.

If the conditions above are satisfied, the income of the non-resident company or trust can be taxed under S739, whether it's UK source income or foreign source income.

Note that one of the above conditions is that the UK resident must have power to enjoy the income of the overseas vehicle (for example, as a shareholder of an overseas company or as a beneficiary of a non-resident trust).

Even if you did not actually receive any income from the trust it is the *potential* to enjoy the income that matters. As such you would not have to actually receive any of the income at all.

Another provision Revenue and Customs could use is S740.

This applies where assets have been transferred abroad and a UK resident other than the settlor obtains a benefit. The beneficiaries then have to pay tax.

In order for this rule to apply the following conditions must be satisfied:

- There must be a transfer of assets.
- As a result of the transfer, income becomes payable to a non-resident person.
- As a result of the transfer, an individual other than the transferor receives a benefit, which is not otherwise subject to tax.
- The person who receives the benefit must be ordinarily resident in the UK.

Section 740 is different from Section 739 in that it taxes *non-transferors* on the benefits they receive.

Benefits which are taxed in terms of Section 740 include payments of any kind, for example cash (capital distributions), the use of property (such as occupation of a house) and interest-free loans.

Where the conditions are satisfied, the individual receiving the benefit is liable to pay tax on the amount or value of the benefit.

It's worth noting that S739 and S740 apply unless you can show that the exemption in S741 applies. In order for this to apply you would need to show that:

- Tax avoidance was not the purpose or one of the purposes for which the transfer took place, or

- The transfer and any associated operations were genuine commercial transactions AND were not designed for the purpose of avoiding tax.

Actually persuading the taxman that you can take advantage of this exemption can in practice be difficult. There are typically two circumstances in which it is applied:

- Firstly, where the purpose of the transaction was the avoidance of *overseas* tax (as opposed to UK tax).

- Secondly, where the settlor is wholly excluded from the settlement. If you were excluded from benefiting from the trust, this would make it much clearer that the purpose of the offshore settlement was not tax driven, given that you would suffer the real economic consequence of losing all possibility of benefiting from your assets.

So there you have it. The CFC rules in whatever guise need to be carefully looked into when considering any form of overseas company or trust.

Use of Foundations

Foundations have become increasingly popular in recent years and offer some of the advantages of trusts while avoiding many of the pitfalls.

Residents of many English-speaking countries view offshore trusts with a certain amount of suspicion. The tax authorities are the most cynical of all and have introduced various pieces of trust-busting legislation over the years.

This has increased the appeal of alternative structures, such as the Private Interest Foundation (PIF).

What is a Foundation?

Foundations are similar to trusts in many ways although there are some crucial differences.

Just like setting up a trust, when an individual sets up a foundation they transfer control over their assets to another person. In other words, the foundation is a separate entity to the settlor.

When a settlor transfers assets to a trust, the trustees hold the assets on behalf of the trust beneficiaries. The trustees are also bound by the trust agreement. However, with a foundation, the foundation itself has a separate legal personality.

As a result the foundation can enter into agreements as it is the owner of the assets which are managed by the foundation council. By contrast a trust is not a separate legal entity different from the trustee (although it is separate from the settlor).

How You Can Use a Foundation

One of the most popular uses for foundations is to hold shares in an international business company (IBC). This puts ownership of the IBC in the hands of a separate legal entity and away from the actual beneficial owner.

Much is made of the benefits that a foundation structure can provide, but essentially the main reason to do this is to demonstrate that the IBC is not controlled by you from your country of residence. Whether this is successful or not in tax terms will likely depend on the anti avoidance rules in your country of residence. In the UK for instance, the foundation is treated for tax purposes in a similar way to a trust. This is not to say that a foundation would not be beneficial for UK residents/domiciliaries, as it could still be a valuable asset protection tool.

If you could navigate the anti-avoidance rules you may then prevent the IBC from being classed as resident in your home country. In the case of the UK this could ensure that the IBC's overseas income and gains are not subject to UK tax.

Most people would use a professional firm to manage and set up such a structure. It makes sense to ensure that the management team are resident in a country other than your own and preferably in a country which has strict privacy laws (such as Liechtenstein or Panama).

A foundation can therefore exist simply as an intermediary, with its main purpose being to take ownership of the company out of your hands so that you are not subject to your country's reporting and tax requirements.

Note that if you are a beneficiary of the foundation, this could then bring you within many countries' anti-avoidance 'trust-busting' rules, with the result that you end up being taxed. Therefore to keep the benefits you should conduct the business of the corporation 'at arm's length'.

In practical terms all day-to-day transactions should be carried out by the IBC on an arm's length basis. For maximum safety you could also consider appointing a professional management firm to be the signatory to the IBC bank account.

Mention this to most people and you can expect a healthy degree of scepticism. After all there's a risk they could take your hard-earned cash and do a moonlight flit.

In reality, provided you use a reputable firm as signatory, this is highly unlikely. Many of the offshore jurisdictions where such firms are located rely on the offshore industry for a lot of their revenues (company registration fees and other taxes). As a result tax haven Governments are keen to protect the reputation of their offshore sectors as much as possible. Strict business confidentiality laws also usually accompany the low taxes.

Many law firms will offer signatory services and this could offer double protection as obtaining such services from a reputable law firm would make it unlikely that a breach of trust would occur. The annual charges for an external signatory range from £500 to £1,500 and therefore whether this is worthwhile may depend on the usage of the account and the value of funds in it.

The benefit of this arrangement is that you enjoy maximum protection and it would be difficult to argue that you control the IBC or foundation, particularly if you also use nominee directors and nominee foundation members. You would be behind the scenes only and would not own or 'control' the assets. Note that although the nominees would control the IBC, you could usually make recommendations to them.

You would, of course, need to set up such a structure after carefully reviewing the tax rules in your home country.

If you are the signatory on an offshore account, many countries such as the US impose some hefty fines for failure to report this.

Another perceived advantage of the foundation and IBC structure is that it can allow traders to avoid paying any tax until they withdraw income or capital gains out of the foundation. The reasoning behind this is that many countries look to whether an offshore corporation is controlled by a resident when deciding if the corporation itself is resident and therefore subject to tax in the home country.

If that taxpayer does not have legal ownership in the company (because the foundation does), many countries' tax rules state that no tax is payable on profits of the company that are not extracted, although obviously they would tax any receipts that came from the company.

There are two caveats here. Firstly, you would need to look at your home country's CFC rules to see if the IBC falls within their scope. If it does, the fact that the profits are not extracted would be irrelevant and they could be taxed in your hands.

Secondly, US citizens have specific rules relating to investment income in such circumstances. If a proportion of the income earned by the IBC is derived from passive investment income, the IRS would take the view that the income would be taxable when earned as opposed to when it's brought back into the country.

This is a pretty unusual view and most countries do not take this stance.

Getting Your Money into the Company

If you're looking to invest some large funds into the IBC/foundation you have to be careful about falling foul of rules relating to gifts in your home country.

For example, the UK, US and many European countries operate gift taxes that could tax a simple transfer of cash or assets (either under inheritance tax or capital gains tax laws).

However, if you obtain something of equal value in return for the transfer there cannot be said to be a 'gift'.

So a transfer in exchange for share capital should not be a gift and could allow the company to be capitalised with minimal tax costs.

In terms of extracting cash one option for getting cash out of the offshore company could be in the form of a loan from the IBC.

In order to keep to the arm's length principle, the loan could be structured in the form of a 'balloon note', which would roll up interest and become payable in a number of years.

Some balloon notes are for 20-year terms and are then renegotiated when the maturity date arrives.

In terms of most offshore IBCs there would be no problem with this. What you would need to look at is whether your home country has any anti-avoidance rules that could effectively tax the loan repayment or, more accurately, the interest element.

Aside from the tax benefits of using the foundation, there are also non-tax benefits including:

- **Privacy.** The privacy benefits are substantial and are one of the key reasons for using the foundation structure. The foundation offers strict confidentiality as regards ownership. Your privacy is easier to protect as you are not usually a beneficiary in any way and would not have any beneficial interest in the foundation assets.

- **Excellent Asset Protection.** Foundations are increasingly used by professionals in high-risk sectors, such as doctors, lawyers, consultants, dentists and accountants, many of whom are at risk of potentially huge liability claims, to protect their assets from creditors.

The key issue here is beneficial ownership. If you own the assets, they would usually be classed as part of your estate and would be available to potential creditors.

However, with a foundation you are no longer the owner of either the beneficial or legal interest in the foundation assets.

This would make it much more difficult for the courts or anyone else to prove that you retained beneficial ownership as the foundation exists completely separately and independently from you and is a separate entity.

It has its own governing council members who direct how the foundation assets will be used.

The IBC/foundation package can also be used for enhanced 'bullet-proof' property protection against creditors.

For example, using a simple company structure an IBC or limited liability company (LLC) could hold the title to some land. A mortgage can be placed on the property by the company, thus absorbing any equity in it. This would make it less attractive to creditors in the case of a lawsuit or dispute.

To make this 'bullet-proof' you could also use a foundation. If it was a US based individual for instance, a Delaware or Nevada LLC would own the land, which would in turn be owned by a separate PIF for asset protection purposes.

When to Use a Foundation

Some of the most common scenarios are:

- Estate planning to pass assets on to children/grandchildren
- To provide for children or other family members
- To protect assets against potential creditors
- To collect royalties
- To invest in the stock market
- As a property investment vehicle
- To operate bank accounts

Best Places to Set Up a Foundation

Not all countries permit a foundation structure. The UK and US for example do not contain foundation provisions within their legislation. There are a variety of countries that offer a foundation including:

- Liechtenstein
- Panama
- Canada
- Luxembourg
- Austria

The most popular locations are Panama and Liechtenstein which get most of the foundation business. The main reason for this is that these are to some extent 'general purpose' foundations that can offer advantages in other jurisdictions as well. By contrast countries such as Canada offer foundations that are particularly suited to Canadian residents.

What to Look for in a Good Foundation

- **Privacy and anonymity**. Panama and Liechtenstein are good choices as they require that the foundation maintains strict secrecy.

- **No taxes**. Both Panama and Liechtenstein can provide zero tax foundations.

116

- **Limited regulation**. You'll probably want to do away with an annual general meeting and the requirement to file annual returns.

- **Cost**. Some jurisdictions have relatively cheap fees with incorporation possible for less than $1,500.

- **Flexibility.** For many it's essential not to be tied to the country where the foundation is established (eg Panama or Liechtenstein).

In essence a foundation offers a separate legal entity with very few restrictions on its use.

This does not eliminate the need to thoroughly review the tax implications in your country of residence but it does allow you to potentially eliminate or reduce any overseas tax implications and conduct your overseas affairs with minimal overseas disclosure.

Using Offshore Companies & Foundations to Save Tax

Most tax havens, including Panama, St Kitts Nevis, the British Virgin Islands and the Bahamas, do not tax their own IBCs on any income generated from business activities conducted outside that jurisdiction (or any capital gains generated from investments outside that country).

You could therefore use such a structure to trade financial assets such as shares, bonds or futures or to hold property or collect royalties and investment income.

A common structure is to use a combination of an IBC, foundation and trust to avoid capital gains tax. In terms of the countries used you could use a Panama foundation coupled with an offshore company established in an overseas jurisdiction (for example, the Bahamas, St Kitts, the BVI, or Cyprus) and an offshore trust established in another jurisdiction such as the Channel Islands.

This would involve an offshore IBC whose shares are owned by a foundation. The trust would then be the sole beneficiary of the foundation and would list all of the beneficiaries.

This structure could allow you to invest overseas (via the offshore IBC) without being subject to capital gains taxes.

The main purpose of the foundation and trust in this arrangement would be to break the ownership link between you and the offshore IBC.

If you owned the offshore IBC directly it would be likely to fall within most countries' CFC rules and, as such, would be subject to tax. The use of the foundation and trust would make it more difficult for the CFC rules to apply. However, your particular domestic tax legislation may contain specific provisions that tackle this – that's why you need to take detailed tax advice from a tax specialist in your home country.

In the UK for instance, although the foundation and trust may help in arguing that the central management and control of the company is not in the UK, you may still face an S739 problem, and this would therefore need to be considered, in particular if you transfer assets to the offshore IBC.

Chapter 6

How an Offshore Company Can Help You

We know that there are lots of different tax havens that can be used to set up an offshore company such as an IBC. But what exactly are the benefits and in what circumstances are offshore companies used?

In the pages that follow I will illustrate the wide variety of uses to which an offshore IBC can be put. If any of these apply to you, the first step should be to obtain advice from a suitably qualified tax specialist.

Trading Companies

With the breaking down of many trading barriers and the ease of international communications, including the growth of the internet, it truly is a global market out there. More businesses are therefore looking to spread their wings and expand overseas.

In these situations, some significant tax-planning benefits can be obtained.

A simple step is to incorporate an offshore company to form part of your trading group. This would principally be used to purchase or resell goods between the group companies.

So international trading companies could use this set up to establish a re-invoicing strategy and accumulate profits in a low-tax jurisdiction.

Common choices to base an offshore trading company would be Cyprus and the Isle of Man in the EU and, further afield, Panama and the Bahamas.

Professional Services Companies

Certain individuals providing professional services often use offshore companies. This is partly for asset protection reasons (they are worried about being sued) and partly for tax-planning purposes.

Such individuals include:

- Lawyers
- Doctors
- Designers
- Consultants
- Entertainers

These individuals can often achieve some considerable tax savings by setting up an offshore company.

How does this work? Well in essence the offshore company can enter into a contract with the individual to provide services for clients outside his country of residence. This could then enable personal income to be accumulated free from tax in the offshore jurisdiction.

If the offshore company was to reinvest the money in a tax-free jurisdiction this could enable future income to be generated free of tax.

Example

Steve, a freelance computer programmer is UK resident and UK domiciled. As a UK resident he'll be taxed in the UK on his worldwide income.

But Steve, being a canny chap, uses a Bahamas IBC to bill some of his clients for work that he actually carries out overseas during his various international contracts.

There are some hoops he'll have to jump through in terms of ensuring that the company does not get classed as a UK-resident company (and therefore itself fall within the UK tax net) and avoiding the anti-avoidance rules. However these can often be overcome and the end result would be that Steve can divert income offshore that would otherwise have been paid to him personally and which then falls outside the scope of UK taxes.

Note that if Steve was to transfer funds to the UK from the offshore company to his personal account (or for his personal benefit) there would then be a UK tax charge.

Using an Offshore Property Company

Investing in property using offshore companies has become increasingly popular as more investors look at investing in overseas property.

The principal advantages of investing via an offshore company are to:

- Avoid inheritance taxes
- Avoid capital gains tax
- Provide the opportunity for a future sale of shares, rather than the underlying property

The procedure is actually remarkably simple. You or the offshore company obtain the funds (usually via a mortgage) which are then used to purchase the property in the name of the IBC.

In terms of you providing funds to the IBC, a straightforward loan would be a good option, depending on the domestic tax legislation. The amount loaned to the IBC could then be extracted tax free in the future.

The rental income would probably not be taxed in the offshore IBC (provided a jurisdiction such as Panama, the Bahamas, or the British Virgin Islands is chosen), however the rental income will often still be taxed in the country where the property is located.

Any tax charge here can usually be minimized by the payment of interest by the IBC, which should be a tax-deductible expense.

Therefore rather than paying cash for a property, the company usually obtains finance for the purchase, from an offshore lender, and the interest payable would further reduce any tax charges.

In the UK using an offshore company to own assets is also popular from an inheritance tax perspective. This is because owning UK assets via an offshore company can enable the UK assets to be taken out of the estate of a non-UK domiciliary.

Example

Elle, a lifelong resident of Canada, is looking to invest in UK investment property. If she purchases the property in her own name this will constitute a UK asset for inheritance tax purposes and, as such, on her death UK probate would be required in addition to a potential tax payment.

If she uses an offshore company to hold the property instead, she will then own shares in an overseas company (a foreign asset) as opposed to a UK property. The shares would not fall into the UK inheritance tax net.

In terms of income tax and capital gains tax, the position of the offshore company would be similar to owning the property personally as a non-resident:

- UK income tax would be levied on the rental profits

- The company would not be taxed on any gain arising when the property is sold.

If you were considering becoming resident in the country where the property is located (for example, retiring there), this will further increase the benefits of using an offshore company to purchase the property before obtaining residence.

By purchasing the property before obtaining residence, it's usually easier to sustain the company's non-resident status and the tax benefits that go with it (in particular, capital gains tax benefits).

If you are both resident and domiciled in the UK, the opportunities to make property investments using offshore companies are more restricted.

Example 2

Let's say Daisy (UK resident and domiciled) wants to buy a property in Bulgaria. She decides to purchase the property via an offshore IBC located in the British Virgin Islands (BVI). The BVI company will own the Bulgarian property but Daisy will own all the shares in the company.

As far as UK tax goes, as a UK domiciliary she would still be subject to UK inheritance tax on her worldwide estate. This would include the Bulgarian property.

If Daisy carefully structures the BVI company so that it is non-UK resident (for example, if she ensures there are overseas directors actually exercising control overseas) the company would be able to dispose of the property free of any UK capital gains tax. Similarly the company would not be subject to income tax on any rental income, as the income is overseas income of a non-resident company.

However as Daisy is UK resident and domiciled, anti-avoidance provisions would apply and any gain on which the company would normally be taxed if it was UK resident will be taxed in her hands.

Similarly, S739 can apply to offshore companies as well as to trusts. This means that the rental income earned by the BVI company could also be taxed in Daisy's hands, unless one of the exemptions applies (for example, if the company is not used to avoid UK tax).

So for UK tax purposes, both UK capital gains tax and income tax could be paid by Daisy on the company's gains and income.

As well as the UK tax, the company will also have to pay Bulgarian withholding taxes on its rental income and capital gains, probably at the rate of 15%.

However, the UK Inland Revenue would allow Daisy to deduct the Bulgarian tax she pays from her UK tax – so the overall effect is that Daisy will be subject to UK tax on all the income and gains of the BVI company.

Of course if she wanted to avoid tax when she sold the property, she could also become non-resident and dispose of the shares in the BVI company. Given that Bulgarian property is typically purchased by non-residents via a company, there could be a good market in such company disposals. As a non-UK resident, Daisy would then be outside the scope of UK CGT, provided her absence abroad lasts for five complete tax years.

Investing or Doing Business in Eastern Europe

Many people are now looking to trade or invest in Eastern Europe, which is braced for a long period of economic growth and development.

A key concern will be extracting cash tax-efficiently from these countries particularly where a locally incorporated company has been used (for local planning or regulatory reasons). The withholding taxes on dividend and interest from East European countries will then be a significant issue.

A popular option here is to establish an offshore company in Cyprus, which has double tax treaties with Bulgaria, the Czech Republic, Hungary, Poland, Romania, Russia and Yugoslavia.

These treaties are pretty unusual in the sense that they are the only treaties the East European countries have with a tax haven country.

We've already looked at the benefits of Cyprus and this is therefore another reason why Cyprus offshore companies are ideal vehicles to extract income such as dividends, interest and royalties from East European countries with minimum tax being paid.

The tax agreements Cyprus has with these countries often stipulate a 0% withholding tax which, combined with the low taxes in Cyprus, makes this a highly effective set up.

Offshore Royalty and Patent Companies

If you have designed a new process or product you could consider using an offshore company. The offshore company could purchase the right to use a patent by you and be given the right to license it to other interested parties.

The offshore company can then enter into agreements with licencees around the world who may then manufacture or otherwise use your patent allowing a tax-free roll-up of funds offshore.

Often royalties paid out of a high-tax area attract withholding taxes at source. In many cases using a holding company may allow a reduction in the amount of tax withheld at source.

Again, Cyprus is another popular EU choice here and a patent could be assigned to a Cyprus offshore company allowing it to exploit the rights and benefit from the nil or 5% withholding tax for royalties stipulated in most of the Cyprus double tax treaties.

Other countries that are popular locations for holding patents and copyrights include The Netherlands, the UK, Madeira, Cyprus and Mauritius.

Avoiding Inheritance Tax

Today's internationally mobile individuals often have properties or other assets located worldwide. A common planning technique is to hold these via an offshore personal investment company. This has advantages that in certain countries (the UK being a prime example) non domiciliaries would not be subject to inheritance tax on the value of the property.

This also has practical benefits in that it ensures that on death the property is passed on in accordance with the deceased's wishes and without long bureaucratic procedures in different countries with different inheritance laws.

It is also much easier to transfer shares in the holding company to the chosen heir. So, in Dubai for instance, in order to avoid any issues of forced succession as regards local property, overseas property investors would typically use a company to purchase the Dubai property, and then leave the shares in the company to their family.

Investment Companies

Using an offshore company could also be considered if you have international investments.

An offshore company can invest funds worldwide. Although generally returns or interest payable are subject to local taxation, there are a number of ways to avoid or greatly reduce the taxation using tax-free bonds, bank deposits that pay interest gross and double tax treaties.

Another aspect for investments will be potential capital gains tax on sale.

Luckily most offshore companies will be exempt from capital gains tax in the tax haven concerned (as practically all the tax havens covered in this book contain some form of CGT exemption).

If you're looking at investing in the EU, you should also see Chapter 9 on the impact of the EU Savings Tax Directive.

Employment Companies

Often, particularly with the growth of e-commerce, there are individuals trading via companies incorporated in a high-tax country who are looking to live offshore.

One option for them to 'have their cake and eat it' is to use an offshore employment company. Using this they would move overseas and become an employee of the offshore IBC. The IBC would charge the trading company in the home country for the services provided (which should be tax deductible) and the IBC would accumulate income-tax free. This could then be extracted by the proprietor.

Multinationals use this on a larger scale and use offshore employment companies as a vehicle to provide expatriate staff, working outside both their home country and the IBC country, with almost tax-free remuneration.

Example

Cedric lives in Spain and owns his own Spanish trading company (Spainco). He has had enough of the high taxes and decides to move to Cyprus, a fellow EU member. Spainco will continue to be subject to Spanish tax, however Cedric can now charge the company a market rate for his services. These payments would be a tax-deductible expense for Spainco.

Assuming Spainco has trading income of €500,000, if it paid €300,000 to Cedric's offshore company (Cyprus IBC) Spainco would then have taxable profits of only €200,000. The €300,000 paid to Cyprus IBC would be subject to significantly lower rates of tax (typically 10%).

Best Places for Offshore Companies

You are literally spoilt for choice when considering where to incorporate your offshore company. The table below looks purely at the tax rates applicable to some of the more popular offshore IBCs.

Country	Corporate tax rate %
Bermuda	0
Cayman Islands	0
Channel Islands	0-20
Isle of Man	10
Cyprus	10
Barbados	1
Vanuatu	0
Bahamas	0
BVI	0
Nevis	0
Anguilla	0
Ireland	12
Gibraltar*	0
Panama*	0

*Note in these countries the 0% rate only applies to foreign-sourced income.

The following is a list of the most popular locations for offshore companies together with the key factors to consider:

Anguilla

- No corporate taxes on company profits
- Tax exempt for 50 years
- No disclosure to tax authorities
- Flexible company name rules

The Bahamas

- No corporate taxes on company profits
- Excellent selection of local professionals
- Long-standing reputation as a stable offshore provider
- No disclosure to tax authorities
- Guaranteed tax exemption for 20 years

Bermuda

- No corporate taxes on company profits
- Does require disclosure to tax authorities
- Investment income derived from abroad may be taxed
- Relatively expensive place to incorporate

British Virgin Islands

- Politically stable and an established corporate destination (over 300,000 IBCs incorporated)
- No corporate taxes for a non-resident company
- No disclosure to tax authorities required
- Fast and low-cost company incorporation

Cayman Islands

- Long-established offshore infrastructure
- Exempt companies pay no corporate taxes
- Exempt for 20 years
- No disclosure to tax authorities
- Strict confidentiality laws

Cyprus

- Full EU member
- Large number of double tax treaties (27 at the last count) which provide for reduced or 0% withholding taxes on dividends, interest and royalties paid to a Cyprus company
- Excellent banking and commercial infrastructure
- Low incorporation and ongoing fees
- Beneficial ownership is disclosed to the Central Bank of Cyprus only, which is bound by secrecy.
- Non-resident companies pay corporate tax at 10% only on income derived in Cyprus

Isle of Man

- Well developed professional and financial infrastructure
- No disclosure to tax authorities
- Exempt companies pay a flat rate of £400 tax per year

Labuan

- One of the leading offshore centres in Asia
- Well-developed financial and professional infrastructure
- No tax for a non-trading exempt company and only 3% or RM20,000 (around $5,000) if the company is trading
- Disclosure to tax authorities required

Liechtenstein

- Politically stable
- Strong banking and financial services
- High levels of privacy and strict confidentiality laws
- Close ties with Switzerland
- Joint stock companies are exempt from income tax, property tax (with the exception for real estate) and capital gains tax.
- No disclosure to tax authorities

St Kitts and Nevis

- The major source of revenue is tourism followed by offshore financial services.
- St Kitts Nevis LLC (limited liability company) can be used for any business venture or professional practice anywhere in the world outside St Kitts.
- Combines the corporate advantages of limited liability with the partnership advantages of pass-through taxation
- No St Kitts tax for non-residents
- No disclosure to tax authorities

Panama

- One of the oldest offshore centres in the world
- Strong secrecy laws
- Minimal reporting requirements
- Bearer shares can be issued
- No tax for non-residents
- No disclosure to tax authorities

Which One is Best?

This is the $64,000 question and, not surprisingly, the answer is not clear cut.

A lot depends on the purpose to which the company is put and the country in which you will be resident.

If you want to trade in China, for example, a Mauritian company could be ideal. If maximum asset protection is required, a St Kitts company is often a good choice because the authorities require a $25,000 bond to be put up before a plaintiff can have a suit filed. This clearly puts off many litigants.

However, overall I would say the best overall offering is the Panamanian IBC. The combination of low set-up expenses, zero taxation and a stable economy is hard to beat.

In addition it offers a guaranteed exemption from Panamanian taxes provided income is derived outside Panama. Other countries

130

such as the Bahamas and Belize offer similar guarantees, however they have limits to the tax-exempt status (typically 15 to 20 years). Panama offers a permanent exemption, which makes it more suitable for long-term tax planning.

Finally, many offshore IBCs have limits as to the business that the IBC can carry out. For example, a Bahamas IBC company cannot engage in business with Bahamians or own property in the Bahamas. By contrast a Panama Company has none of these problems.

Step by Step Guide to Setting Up Your IBC

You will almost certainly use an incorporation agent who will take care of all the paperwork for you. However, you too need to know about the various procedures involved so you understand exactly what is happening and what you are signing.

The information below is a general guide. The actual procedure and what you can and cannot do will vary between tax havens (for example, as to whether bearer shares can be issued, the minimum number of directors and whether you can use nominees).

However, the following list will give you a useful insight into how a company is set up:

Step 1
The first step will be choosing the country in which to form your IBC. Hopefully, after reading this book, you will have some idea as to which country is best for you. You'll have to take into account not just the tax environment of your chosen country but also what the company will be used for, the setup and ongoing costs, and privacy and confidentiality issues.

Step 2
Next, you'll need to think about the type of entity that you want to form. Many offshore jurisdictions will offer different types of IBC companies, for example exempt companies, non-resident companies, holding companies, as well as other entities such as LLPs and LLCs.

With respect to IBCs the key differences will usually be in terms of filing requirements and annual fees but you should ask your incorporation agent about the differences between the various types of entity.

Step 3
Next you will need to choose your company's name. You've got pretty much a free rein here although you'll need to be guided by your incorporation agent to ensure that the name does not break any restrictions in the country of incorporation. Note that if you form a ready made company, you will need to change the name of the company to one that you want.

Step 4
Next the articles of association will need to be drafted. These are basically the rules that govern the operation of the company and are often provided by your incorporation agent in the form of standard pro forma documents. You could however draft customized ones if preferred. However for most people the standard articles should be fine.

Step 5
You will then need to think about the share capital and method of funding. When you form your company you may need to transfer some money into the company. There are essentially two different ways to do this, either as a loan or as share capital. The advantage of a loan is that it allows a tax-free extraction of funds in the future by way of a loan repayment.

Note that many developed countries (for example, the UK) have special rules (known as 'thin capitalisation' rules) that prevent overseas individuals forming companies with low share capital and large loans.

Because interest on loans is tax deductible, but dividends on shares are not, overseas companies could gain an easy tax advantage by forming UK subsidiaries with large loan accounts. The taxman therefore restricts the tax deductibility of interest unless the debt/equity ratio of the company is realistic (in other words, would a third party bank lend the funds to the company in question?)

When we're looking at share capital usually the amount that you initially subscribe is low (for example, $100) and this nominal share capital bears no relation to the underlying value of the company.

For example, a $1 share could easily be worth $10,000 – the value of the share will depend on the level of assets and profitability of the company.

Step 6

There are various types of shares (or, more correctly, classes of share) that could be issued by the company and you'll need to decide which shares your company will issue.

These include:

Bearer shares – These are shares that give the holder of the share certificate the rights of ownership. In theory if you lose the share certificates you would then lose the ownership over those shares.

The benefit in issuing bearer shares is that there is no disclosure of the real owner's name in the shareholders' register. This makes bearer shares ideal where anonymity is important.

In practice, bearer share certificates aren't issued in many non-offshore jurisdictions (and where they are, the share certificates are usually kept in a locked safe). So bearer shares are not permitted in the UK, US, Australia, Cyprus and Singapore. All shares in these jurisdictions must be registered. Many jurisdictions do, however, permit bearer shares, including:

- Anguilla
- The British Virgin Islands
- The Cayman Islands
- Switzerland
- Liechtenstein
- Panama
- Malta
- The Bahamas
- Austria
- Germany
- Costa Rica

The advantage of bearer shares is that they offer excellent privacy. However, the same rights and responsibilities apply to this type of share as to any other and just because the shares are held as bearer shares doesn't alter the tax position. You would still be liable to tax on either any dividends received or on a gain on disposal, subject to the tax rules of your country of residence.

Preference shares – These usually offer the shareholder a fixed dividend receipt paid in preference to ordinary shareholders. They do not usually give owners the right to vote on company affairs.

Class A & B shares – Having different classes of share allows you to give different rights and benefits to different groups of shareholders.

You could, for example, grant class A shares to be held by you with full voting and dividend rights and class B shares with no voting rights but full dividend rights to be held by someone else. These could be gifted or subscribed for by your children, allowing an entitlement to income with no influence on the operation of the company.

Step 7
Of crucial importance is deciding who will be the directors of the company. You'll need to ensure that the minimum number of directors is met (usually 2-3). Often it will be you and your wife or other family members/business partners who will be acting as directors.

If you're looking at establishing an offshore IBC you may need to consider using the services of nominees to act as directors.

A lot of the offshore incorporation agents will try and convince you to use them for this purpose. Aside from the fact that they will charge you for this service, you need to realise that they will have control over your company.

If you're keen to establish that the company is controlled from overseas a good option is to arrange for the company to be owned by an offshore trust, with control passed to a professional trust management company.

You could then be a beneficiary of the trust and, provided the trust exercised control overseas, the company could be argued to be non-resident.

If required, the trustees could even act as directors of the company. This would make it easier to establish the company as non-resident.

How Long Does it Take to Set Up a Company?

This will depend on the country in question and will vary from between one week and one month.

You'll often be offered an off-the-shelf corporation as a fast option. You need to be careful here as you do not know the company's history. In other words, whether the company was engaged in something that will come back to bite you later on.

Given that the incorporation process is usually pretty straightforward it usually makes sense to incorporate from scratch.

How Much Does it Cost to Set Up an Offshore Company?

As you'd expect, the cost will vary tremendously depending on which country you choose and which incorporation agent you use. You'll be looking at an IBC in Costa Rica or Panama for as little as £500. By contrast, incorporating in Bermuda will cost you several thousand pounds.

You need to be careful as there are a number of offshore formation firms and lawyers that charge outrageous amounts of money to set up and maintain both foundation, trust and IBC structures. Some of these prices are way out of line but most people do not know any better and end up paying quite a bit.

As with everything, do your research before committing yourself.

Chapter 7

How Big Companies and the Rich Use Tax Havens

Tax havens are also of great use to companies, as well as individuals. In fact, some of the world's largest multinationals such as Pepsi and News International use offshore tax haven structures to minimize the overall amount of tax they pay.

Of course, the big multinationals have teams of highly paid tax advisers whose job it is to ferret out tax-saving opportunities around the globe. Broadly speaking there are two distinct ways they use tax havens to slash a company's overall tax rate.

This overall tax rate (also known as the effective tax rate) is simply the total tax paid by the company divided by its profits.

The first way they reduce their taxes is by 'corporate migration'. The second way is by using tax haven subsidiaries.

Corporate Migration

This is the most straightforward option and at its most simple means that a company transfers its headquarters to an offshore tax haven. This could either be a total transfer of operations, a part transfer of operations or sometimes the transfer would be in name only without the actual operations being moved.

You'll need to be careful when doing this, as many developed countries won't be fooled by a transfer in name only. You would actually need to transfer physical operations, which in itself could lead to a further tax charge.

In practice what you often see is a part transfer of operations with, for example, back-office functions and even some front line services (for example, call centres and customer services functions) being transferred overseas.

The tax savings come about because in many tax havens companies do not have to pay taxes on their overseas operations. As always, detailed professional advice is required to ensure that the residence of the company is actually transferred.

Using Tax Haven Subsidiaries

This is really where the teams of tax accountants that the large multinationals have on tap come into their own.

The use of offshore subsidiaries is big business – Enron, for example had over 600, many just existing in name only.

This is a complex area and the uses of these companies will obviously depend on the jurisdictions involved, types of business and so on. However, as an illustration here are some of the most popular strategies:

Deferring Tax Payments

A number of countries, such as the US, tax resident companies on their worldwide profits but also allow a deferral of tax for any profits generated from overseas operations, provided the profits are reinvested overseas. This therefore allows corporate groups based in these countries to use tax haven subsidiaries to hold overseas trading operations and reduce the overall tax charge.

Income Stripping/Offshore Finance Companies

This idea is developed below but essentially involves a tax haven subsidiary lending money to a tax paying company. The interest charged on the loans is then allowable as a tax deduction for the tax paying company but should be subject to low or no tax in the tax haven company.

Offshore Intellectual Property

Similar to the above, a tax paying company would transfer intellectual property (this is a very wide term and includes patents, copyright, know-how and goodwill) to a tax haven subsidiary. The tax haven company can then charge a licensing fee for the use of the intellectual property.

The income from any overseas subsidiaries that pay the tax haven company for using the intellectual property would then not be taxable in the hands of the tax paying company.

In addition, and in a similar way to income stripping above, the tax haven company can charge the tax paying company and these charges should be tax deductible for the tax paying company (a double benefit arises as there would be both a tax deduction on payment and no tax payable on receipt).

Transfer Pricing

This used to be a major opportunity but some of the larger industrialised countries now have strict transfer-pricing legislation.

Transfer pricing simply means the rate charged for good and services between connected parties, such as between a parent company and subsidiaries.

The aim with any effective transfer pricing strategy would be to arrange the group structure so that tax paying companies are paying management charges or other inter-company service charges to tax haven group companies. Provided the paying company gets a tax deduction for the amount paid, the group would be significantly better off.

This would typically also apply to purchases of stock or parts from overseas or intercompany salaries charged for using overseas staff. The mark-up would enable an increased tax deduction for the company that pays the management charge in the high tax country.

Note that it's essential that the paying company gets a tax deduction for the payments in order for this to be tax effective.

Nowadays companies need to be careful that transfer pricing legislation does not apply to require an arm's length rate to be used. The UK, for example, has some strict transfer-pricing provisions that will effectively only allow a tax deduction in these circumstances for the market value of the services provided. If this applied it would then negate the benefit of the high transfer price.

Using Holding Companies

Holding companies are often used as a form of financial funnel. By having a company located in a suitable holding company jurisdiction hold the shares in a variety of companies, it's possible to ensure that the profits are funnelled into a low tax, or tax advantageous environment.

In order to be effective there are a number of prerequisites that a holding company and subsidiary must satisfy, in particular an ability to avoid withholding taxes.

Ability to Avoid Withholding Taxes & CGT

Most developed countries impose some type of withholding tax on dividends, interest or royalties sent overseas by companies.

This usually works a bit like PAYE for employees. When an employee receives salary an amount has already been deducted and paid to the tax authorities by the employer. In other words, the payer has accounted for tax on behalf of the recipient.

The same applies to withholding taxes. The payer company will complete any required forms and withhold tax from the payment on behalf of the recipient.

The recipient who has suffered the withholding tax will need to look at the domestic tax legislation to identify whether any tax relief can be claimed.

Some countries such as the UK and the US automatically allow a measure of relief for any overseas tax paid when calculating the recipient's local tax liability. This is where double tax treaties really come in handy. Certain treaties will allow payments between participating states to be made free of withholding tax or at least at reduced rates.

This could therefore allow dividends, interest and royalties to be passed between the holding company and subsidiary companies without any tax being deducted. Of course, there may be tax on the receipt of the dividend in the holding company, depending on the local tax regime.

"Why not then base the holding company in a tax haven to avoid all taxes?" is a question many people ask. Well, in principle this is sound, the problem is that most tax haven countries do not have any double tax treaties, and where they do they are not the standard OECD treaty giving withholding tax relief. Therefore you would be subject to the full rates of withholding taxes.

The trick therefore is to find a country that has the tax treaty benefits with a favourable domestic tax regime for the holding company.

Another point to bear in mind is capital gains tax (CGT). The holding company will be doing just that – holding shares in a variety of subsidiary companies. What if someone comes along and offers to buy one of the subsidiary companies?

The holding company needs to ensure that it's not located in a regime that is going to tax it heavily on the capital gain. Therefore any profits attributable to the holding company when it sells any subsidiaries should be subject to no (or low) taxes.

Another issue mainly for the large multinationals is that the holding company may simply itself be an intermediate company. You may, for example, have the following corporate structure:

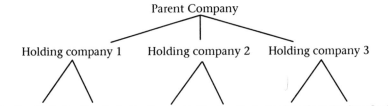

In this case, holding companies 1, 2 and 3 are all holding companies but they are themselves owned by the parent company (the 'top' company is sometimes known as the 'ultimate holding company').

This is a common structure for multinational groups mainly because the structure of the group can be aligned with the geographical location of the businesses or according to the industries the group operates in. So, for example, Holding Company 1 may hold all the companies trading in Europe, Holding Company 2 may hold all the companies trading in the US, and so on. Alternatively, Holding Company 1 may hold the trading companies involved in the manufacture of widgets, while the other holding companies own shares in trading companies involved in other industries.

You'll therefore see a flow of cash from the trading companies to the holding companies and finally up to the parent company in the form of dividends or by way of other charges (for example, royalties or management charges).

Anyone using such a structure would need to ensure firstly that dividends paid by a holding company to the parent company are either exempt from or subject to low withholding tax in the holding company's jurisdiction. Secondly, low or zero capital gains tax on disposal of the shares by the parent company would be important.

Seeing that one of the main attractions of a holding company is its ability to receive dividend payments with little or no tax deducted and that typical tax haven companies often do not fit this purpose (due to the lack of double tax treaties), which countries are the best place to locate holding companies?

Denmark

Denmark is a highly attractive location for holding companies. Being part of the EU, it's subject to the EU's Parent-Subsidiary directive. This means that where a Danish holding company controls at least 25% of the shares of another EU subsidiary, any dividends paid by the subsidiary to the Danish holding company will not have withholding tax deducted.

As a back-up, Denmark also has lots of double tax treaties (approximately 80 in fact) to reduce the rates of withholding tax on dividends received by Danish holding companies from non-EU countries, or where the EU directive doesn't apply.

Avoiding withholding taxes is just one aspect. Of crucial importance is the tax treatment in Denmark itself. The Danish corporate income tax rate is 30% but there is special legislation that exempts dividends received by a Danish holding company, provided various conditions are satisfied. Where this applies there's no tax in Denmark, even if tax has not been paid by the subsidiary that paid the dividend.

This makes Denmark unusual in the EU as the other key holding company jurisdictions (Austria, Belgium, France, Germany, Luxembourg, The Netherlands and the UK) only exempt the dividend income if the foreign subsidiary has already paid tax.

In terms of capital gains tax on the sale of shares by the holding company, the standard CGT rate in Denmark can be up to almost 60%. However, again the domestic legislation contains an exemption which can ensure that no CGT is charged on the gains that a holding company makes when it disposes of an overseas subsidiary.

Therefore, Denmark offers a highly attractive regime for locating a holding company and is often considered the benchmark offshore holding company jurisdiction.

In terms of tax on dividend income, the combination of Denmark's double tax treaty network and its holding company regime means that it offers some serious advantages and there are currently approximately 35 countries which can route their dividends through Denmark without paying any withholding taxes. This combined with the CGT exemption means it is one of the top holding company destinations.

Belgium

Belgium is another popular location for holding companies. The principal advantage is on the capital gains tax front. Where a Belgian holding company disposes of shares in a subsidiary, the gain it realises can be completely exempt from Belgian CGT. This is similar to the position of Danish holding companies, however in actual fact it's even more beneficial. This is because the Danish holding companies are subject to more restrictions that do not apply to Belgian companies (for example, the holding company would need to hold the shares for at least three years).

142

United Kingdom

The UK is often overlooked as a holding country location, although it does offer some excellent opportunities.

For a start the UK has more double tax treaties than all of its main competitors. Given the quality and extent of the treaty network, it is often said to be the best country for extracting overseas dividends at the lowest tax cost.

The UK will also allow the shareholder to claim a tax credit for any 'underlying tax'. This is the tax the company has already paid before paying the dividend (for example, the company's corporation tax charge). In order to claim credit for underlying tax, the shareholder must own at least 10% of the shares in the company.

This therefore means that where the underlying foreign corporate tax rate is 30% or more, this credit will normally mean total relief from UK corporation tax. So it's therefore effectively the same as an exemption in these circumstances. Also bear in mind that the UK has lower rates of corporation tax than most other industrial nations.

The UK is also pretty unusual in that it doesn't impose any withholding tax on dividends distributed by UK companies to UK non-resident shareholders. So non-resident shareholders can usually extract funds from a UK company free of UK income tax.

There are also capital gains tax benefits to UK holding companies. Where they are part of a trading group, new substantial shareholding legislation should apply to exempt any gain arising in full.

Finally, it's also very cheap to set up and run a UK holding company.

How Can You Use the Offshore Holding Company?

It's all very well learning how multinationals benefit from offshore holding companies. But if you're looking at establishing an international business, how can you take advantage of these opportunities?

Some of the possibilities are as follows:

Offshore Finance Company

A common use of the offshore company is as a provider or funds.

If you're looking at establishing a business to trade in the EU or USA for example, you could use an offshore holding company that would provide funds to subsidiaries in various countries so that the subsidiaries obtain the benefit of tax deductions on interest paid.

This is effectively a way of creating a tax deduction that may not otherwise be available. Note you would need to be careful to ensure that any loan was correctly drafted (for example, using suitable loan agreements) and the interest rate is calculated on an arm's length basis.

Example

You've designed a new widget and will be selling it around the world. As well as establishing suitable trading companies onshore, you could take advantage of an offshore holding company to fund the initial set up as follows:

The holding company would obtain the funds (either from a bank or investors) and would lend the funds to the trading subsidiaries. They would then use the funds for the purpose of their trade (for example, the manufacture and sale of new widgets).

144

Ideally the holding company would be situated offshore in an area where there is no corporation tax and this would allow it to roll up funds tax free. The trading companies should also be entitled to a tax deduction for the interest paid to the holding company, provided this is structured correctly.

This is a win-win scenario as there is a tax deduction, with no corresponding taxable receipt.

Interest payments from group companies may be subject to withholding tax, but these taxes differ from the usual corporation taxes. Many large companies establish their own offshore companies for the purpose of mixing dividends of subsidiaries and deriving maximum advantage from tax credits. This 'pooling' or 'mixing' of income is a complex area and is something that in house tax departments of multinationals look at in considerable detail.

Offshore Patent Holding

If you've designed a new process or product you could consider using an offshore company. The offshore company could purchase the right to use your patent and sublicense it.

The offshore company can then enter into agreements with licensees around the world who may then manufacture or otherwise use your patent allowing a tax-free roll up of funds in the offshore company.

Royalties paid out of a high-tax country often attract withholding taxes at source but in many cases using a holding company may allow a reduction in the rate of tax withheld at source.

Note that the offshore company should acquire the patent as soon as possible to ensure that little value is attributed to it. If possible it should be assigned/sold while still pending, as a gain may well arise on the transfer to the company. If the patent holder is based in a high tax jurisdiction this could represent a substantial gain arising, particularly if the transfer to the overseas company is deemed to be at market value (which would be the case in most high-tax jurisdictions).

Minimizing Risk

This is based on the 'don't place all your eggs in one basket' principle. As some countries suffer from both political and economic instability you may like to follow the example of many large multinationals that move the base of operations and ownership of assets offshore. If you're looking for a sound environment, with excellent political stability, some of the Caribbean jurisdictions may not be top choice. Places like Luxembourg or Bermuda are the favoured jurisdictions.

Avoidance of CGT and Withholding Taxes

As you've seen above, one of the main uses of offshore holding companies is to extract profits free of withholding taxes and CGT.

You may be considering investing or trading in a country with which your home country does not have a double tax treaty.

In this case, you may decide to use a holding company in a jurisdiction that does have a suitable double tax treaty. For example, Cyprus has an extensive double tax treaty network with many Eastern European countries and countries of the former Soviet Union, and the use of Cypriot companies for inward investment into these countries is often advised.

You'll need to be careful though, as a number of double tax treaties, in particular US treaties, now have 'limitation of benefits' articles which can restrict treaty benefits (see Chapter 10 on double tax treaties).

Chapter 8

Protecting Your Privacy with Nominees

Using an IBC as a nominee or for re-invoicing purposes are two common uses for offshore companies, so it's worthwhile looking into them in a little more detail.

A nominee arrangement is not really in itself a tax-saving option, although the privacy benefits would mean it could be used in conjunction with other tax-planning structures.

The basic premise is that one of the disadvantages of using an offshore IBC is that the tax authorities in some of the high-tax developed countries may pay close attention to your Cayman Islands or Panamanian IBC.

However, by using a company in an 'onshore' jurisdiction you are less likely to raise suspicion. Of course, there should be nothing to hide in the first place but often it's a case of avoiding long protracted tax enquiries.

This arrangement is really only suitable for a trader.

How Does it Work?

Well, taking the UK as an example, a UK company is incorporated to be used as the nominee company. The UK company acts on behalf of an offshore IBC which is itself based in a tax haven.

This is basically an agency arrangement with the UK company being the 'agent' and the offshore IBC being the 'principal'. Therefore any business that the UK company conducts is on behalf of the tax haven IBC.

The type of activities the UK company could get involved in would include negotiating deals, marketing, administration and so on. The UK company could invoice UK clients for services performed and then pay the cash received to the tax haven company, less a small charge for the services provided.

The tax haven company is effectively kept out of the trading operations and for all intents and purposes the clients deal directly with the UK company. This may also reassure any client companies that may otherwise not want to deal with a tax haven company.

Note that in order for this to be a proper commercial arrangement, the agency company should charge a fee to the tax haven IBC for the provision of its services, and in its accounts the amount of trading income handled on behalf of the offshore IBC would not normally have to be shown.

Given the strict transfer pricing laws in many countries the amount of the fee would need to be carefully considered and based on a market rate – as a rough guide 5% to 15% of the gross turnover. Any expenses of the agency company are set against this and tax will be paid in the UK on the taxable profits.

The cash could then be extracted by any non-resident shareholders free of UK income taxes.

The benefit of this arrangement is that a resident company is less likely to be subject to scrutiny than an offshore company based in a tax haven. Clearly if any enquiries are made by the tax authorities the arrangement should be fully disclosed and provided an arm's length basis is used and adequate documentary evidence is retained to back up the nominee structure, this should alleviate any concerns.

When Can the Agency Structure Be Used?

Trading operations

This type of arrangement is most relevant to a trading operation and effectively separates the transactions, with the invoicing being done by the agency company and delivery and transfer of title in the goods resting with the offshore IBC.

Note that it's important to distinguish between the invoicing and the generation of profit. Whereas there is no problem with the nominee company invoicing for the services or products provided, any profit actually made should be generated by the tax haven 'principal' company.

Therefore the offshore IBC should actually purchase and dispose of the goods (for example, transfer title) to ensure that any profit is made by the IBC. Provided you've chosen the location of the offshore IBC carefully, no tax should be payable by the IBC. You should also bear in mind that most IBCs aren't allowed to trade in the country where they are incorporated.

Property

You could also use this structure for owning property. In this case the offshore IBC would own the property and the agency company would act as a property management agent.

Rental income is invoiced by the nominee company and received by it on behalf of the offshore IBC. As above, the agency company would charge a commercially acceptable fee to the IBC (calculated on an arm's length basis) which would usually be taxable (less expenses).

The benefits here are that:

- The tenants don't know they are dealing with an offshore IBC.

- Any gain on disposal would arise in the offshore IBC (for example, in the case of the UK, any gain would be exempt if the offshore company is non-UK resident).

- The rental income would be taxed in the hands of the IBC.

Service companies

The agency structure could also be used where you are supplying services via an offshore company but didn't want these invoices shown in your accounts. This may be the case where for example you move offshore and invoice your trading company for services you provide.

Your customers

If you are based offshore and provide services to client companies possibly in a high tax jurisdiction, your customers may not like having invoices from a tax haven in their accounts on the basis that the taxman may look into their affairs in a bit more detail.

You could therefore form an agency company in a respectable 'onshore' jurisdiction (for example, the UK) to invoice the client.

Where to Incorporate

This will clearly depend on the use of the agency arrangement and the countries of any trading/property holding.

However, the UK is known as a good choice for the nominee company, given its sound trading reputation and tough anti-money-laundering rules.

In terms of the offshore company – take your pick! The Bahamas, British Virgin Islands and Panama are all favourites.

As you'll see, closely linked with the nominee idea, is the use of a company as a tool for re-invoicing.

Re-invoicing is just the establishment of an offshore IBC to act as an intermediary between a trader and the clients.

It allows profits to be split between onshore and offshore jurisdictions, with the aim obviously being to redirect some of the trading profits to tax haven jurisdictions. Profits could then be accumulated offshore, with hopefully (if structured correctly) the onshore company receiving a tax deduction for the amounts paid to the offshore company.

Example

An international trading company sells €1,000,000 of goods to European customers and earns a gross profit €400,000. It pays tax at 30%, so its tax bill will be €120,000 reducing its net profits to €280,000.

One option the company may consider would be to establish a tax haven IBC to act as intermediary. The trader sells its products to the tax haven IBC on paper for, say, €800,000. The tax haven IBC would then sell the goods to the eventual customers for

€1,000,000. The tax haven IBC would therefore show a profit of €200,000 but assuming it's a 0% tax haven there should be no tax charge.

The trading company would realize a profit of €200,000 as it sold the goods for €800,000 and incurred costs of €600,000.

The use of a re-invoicing strategy would save the trading company being taxed on €200,000, which could equate to a tax saving of €60,000.

Where is the Re-invoicing Company Incorporated?

The re-invoicing company is usually formed in one of the Caribbean tax haven jurisdictions (often combined with a nominee company incorporated in a less high-profile environment). So you'd be looking at the British Virgin Islands, the Bahamas, St Kitts Nevis etc, given that they provide a sound tax environment for import/export companies.

The main problem with this type of scheme is transfer pricing. The disposal by a trading company to the re-invoicing company is traditionally at a discount to allow a profit to be made overseas. In countries with strong transfer pricing requirements, this would need to be justified (for example because of additional services still to be provided by the re-invoicing company). Given that transfer pricing is a specialist area, it is essential that specific advice from a suitable specialist is obtained.

This is not the only problem with this reinvoicing strategy – remember the anti-avoidance rules that we looked at earlier? Well in this case the tax haven IBC could easily be classed as a controlled foreign company if it falls foul of the CFC conditions (for example, for US tax purposes if its shares are owned by US residents). This would result in the profits of the tax haven IBC being subject to tax along with the international trading company. For this reason, reinvoicing is a difficult strategy to get passed the tax authorities, although you'll need to take detailed advice on the implications for your particular country of residence.

Chapter 9

How to Avoid the EU Savings Tax Directive

This has the potential to be a huge blow to EU residents having offshore bank accounts. As part of the EU's attempt to crack down on tax evasion, the EU Savings Tax Directive (ESD) was implemented as from 1 July 2005.

The ESD is an agreement between the member States of the EU to automatically exchange information with each other about customers who earn savings income in one EU member sate but actually reside in another.

Put simply, this means that if you live in the EU and have a bank account in any other EU country, details of you and the interest you earn will be passed to the tax authorities in your home country, who will undoubtedly check that you've been entering the information on your tax return. If you've not been declaring it, as a minimum they'll be likely to look for payment of the outstanding tax and interest, along with penalties.

Three of the EU states kicked up a fuss about this and have chosen to pull out. Austria, Belgium and Luxembourg have opted to apply alternative arrangements for the time being.

Under these alternative arrangements, tax will be deducted at source from income earned by EU resident individuals on savings held in other EU countries.

Therefore under this option banks will automatically deduct tax from interest and other savings income earned and pass it to their local tax authority, indicating how much of the total amount relates to customers in each member state.

The rate of withholding tax will be 15% from 1st July 2005, 20% from 1st July 2008 rising to 35% from 1st July 2011.

It's important to remember that states that go for the withholding tax option do so as an alternative to exchanging information. As such, the member state receiving the payments receives a bulk payment but does not receive personal details in respect of each individual. This will preserve confidentiality of customers overseas accounts.

As well as Austria, Belgium and Luxembourg opting for a withholding tax, a number of other countries have also now gone down this route (to preserve banking secrecy) including:

- Switzerland
- The Turks and Caicos Islands
- Liechtenstein
- The Isle of Man
- The British Virgin Islands
- Andorra

Even if you have an account in an overseas jurisdiction that applies the withholding option, you could if you wished 'contract out' of the withholding tax option and agree to the exchange of information with your country of residence.

Note that non UK domiciliaries are effectively exempt from the directive and they would usually need to apply to Revenue & Customs for a certificate to give to the overseas bank to ensure there is no withholding tax deducted (or exchange of information).

Which Countries Are Affected

The ESD will apply to all EU member states. Great, you're thinking, I'll keep my cash in a Caribbean tax haven, and avoid any withholding taxes.

Unfortunately, it is not that simple. Although the legal scope of the directive cannot extend outside the EU, its implementation will also affect:

- UK Crown Dependencies
- UK Overseas Territories
- Dependent Territories of The Netherlands
- Other 'Third Countries' that have volunteered to opt in

Whilst most of the EU members have gone for the exchange of information option, most of the others have opted for the withholding tax (on the basis it will do least damage to the offshore industry).

The table below shows which countries have opted for which option.

Withholding tax option	Exchange of info option
Channel Islands	UK
Isle of Man	Ireland
Belgium	France
Luxembourg	Germany
Austria	Italy
British Virgin Islands	Spain
Turks and Caicos Islands	Portugal
Switzerland	Greece
Andorra	Sweden
Liechtenstein	Finland
	Denmark
	Cyprus
	Czech Republic
	Estonia
	Hungary
	Monaco
	Latvia
	Lithuania
	Malta
	Poland
	Slovakia and Slovenia
	Anguilla
	Cayman Islands
	Montserrat

You'll see from the above that some of the EU's own low tax jurisdictions, notably Cyprus, Gibraltar and Malta will be exchanging information on interest receipts from EU residents.

In addition, the Caribbean tax havens of the Cayman Islands, Anguilla and Montserrat will also be exchanging information. This should come as no big hiccup if your overseas interest income is already being correctly declared in your tax return. Also some of the key tax havens such as Bermuda, Panama and the Bahamas are not included in the provisions.

Will the ESD Affect You?

If you are an individual who is resident in an EU member state and earn bank interest or other savings income on investments held in one of the countries identified above, then it is likely that you will be affected by the directive and will either be subject to the withholding tax or the exchange of information.

How Can the Terms of the Directive Be Avoided?

There are a number of ways that the obligations imposed by the directive could be avoided. In other words, where there would be no requirement to deduct a withholding tax or exchange information with your home state:

- Invest your cash in a bank account in a country not listed above and one in which another automatic exchange of information agreement is not in place.

  This could include: Labuan, Panama, Hong Kong, America, the Bahamas, Bermuda, Antigua and St Kitts and Nevis.

- Become a non-EU resident and you can invest your cash anywhere you want. The ESD will then not apply to any income earned from your investments.

- The ESD only applies to 'individuals'. One option if you are an EU resident would be to use a company (either onshore or offshore) to make the investments. The company would then not be subject to the terms of the ESD and the rules of your domestic regime would apply. If an offshore IBC was used, perhaps in conjunction with an offshore trust or foundation, you would need to review your domestic tax regime to ascertain whether you had any filing responsibilities.

- The ESD only applies to 'interest payments'. This is drafted widely to include 'debt claims of every kind'. This will therefore include income from

Government securities
Bonds or debentures
Accrued and capitalized interest

The big omission here is that it won't apply to dividends from shares or capital gains.

Therefore careful choosing of investments could literally reap dividends! Investing in overseas equities as opposed to cash would avoid the terms of the ESD and you could also consider an investment bond with an offshore insurance company which would also be outside the scope of the ESD. In some EU countries, including the UK, this can also offer other tax benefits including a reduction in income tax.

Chapter 10

The Tremendous Benefits of Double Tax Treaties

Double tax treaties offer some substantial benefits to individuals and businesses that have international income.

A double tax treaty (DTT) is essentially an agreement between two countries that determines which country has the right to tax you in specified situations. The purpose behind this is to avoid double taxation.

It would be easy for a resident of one country to have income that arises in a second country. In this case both countries may want to tax the income (country 1 on the residence basis and country 2 on the source basis). This is where a DTT may come into play.

A treaty may state, for example, that certain types of capital gains should only be taxed in the country of residence, as opposed to the country where the asset is located. Or it may specifically provide for tax paid in one country to be deducted from the tax bill in another country.

However, the potential benefits of double tax treaties go far beyond this simple example.

What the Typical DTT Provisions Really Mean

I don't know if you've ever looked at a double tax treaty but they can be extremely difficult to follow. Most of the UK DTTs follow the standard OECD formula and below I've highlighted some of the most common provisions.

Some of the provisions are self explanatory but are worth stating in case you ever want to review a tax treaty on your own.

The first couple of articles usually look at what taxes the treaty will apply to and define any terms that are to be used.

Article I - Taxes Covered

It's always worthwhile checking that the tax you're interested in is expressly stated in this section. It will say here exactly which taxes in both states the treaty applies to. So, for example, the UK-Cyprus treaty states that it covers income tax and corporation tax in the UK and just income tax in Cyprus (no mention of capital gains tax). On the other hand, the UK-France treaty covers UK income tax, capital gains tax and corporation tax, along with French income and corporation tax.

Note that you won't find inheritance tax covered in these treaties. Inheritance tax treaties are completely separate and quite rare.

It's from Article IV onwards though that you'll find the really important stuff.

Article IV – Residence

This article will determine where you are resident for tax purposes if you are a resident of two or more countries under the domestic tax laws of the countries concerned (this is commonly referred to as the 'treaty tie-breaker rules').

The OECD model treaty provides that:

- If you have a permanent home in one state, you are resident in that state.
- If you have a permanent home in both states, you are resident in the state which is your 'centre of vital interests' – the country in which you have close personal and financial ties.
- If you do not have a permanent home in either state and it is not possible to determine your centre of vital interests, you are resident in the country where you have an 'habitual abode'.

So, if you are a resident of two countries based on their domestic rules, you would look at these tests to find out which country you are 'treaty resident' in to determine which country has the right to tax you.

Article V – Permanent Establishment

This looks at the definition of a permanent establishment. This is crucial for international traders as it will frequently dictate the extent to which overseas trading activities will be taxed in an overseas jurisdiction. We'll look at this in a bit more detail shortly.

Article VI – Income from Real Property

Typically real property is land and property, so this article would cover the treatment of rental income. In practically all treaties the source country (where the property is located) is given the right to tax rental income from the property, along with the country of residence. As no exemption is provided in the treaty, relief from double tax will usually be given by way of a tax credit for any overseas tax paid.

Article XI – Interest

This article looks at the position where interest is paid by a resident of one country to a resident of another. The treaty between the two countries would usually look to either reduce any withholding taxes paid in the country where the interest is paid from, or state that the interest is exempt in the country of source.

Article XIII – Capital Gains

This is the article that is of most importance for property investors looking to emigrate and sell up. It covers capital gains from the disposal of assets. In many cases there is a catch-all provision that capital gains remain taxable ONLY in the seller's country of residence, except for land which can also typically be taxed in the country where the land is located.

Article XIV – Independent Personal Services

This article looks at the taxation of income earned by self-employed people. If an individual has a 'fixed base' in another country, that country may tax any income that arises directly from that fixed base in a similar way that a business is taxed on profits from overseas permanent establishments.

Article XV – Dependent Personal Services

This looks at the taxation of employment income. In many treaties if the income is paid by a foreign employer and the employee is not physically present in the UK for more than 183 days, the income will only be taxable in the employee's country of residence.

Article XXIV – Elimination of Double Taxation

This allows what is already incorporated into UK tax law: the foreign tax credit.

This article is a catch-all that prevents double taxation with respect to income not addressed above and allows a deduction for overseas tax paid.

Article XXVII – Exchange of Information

This article is an agreement between the tax authorities to swap information to prevent tax evasion.

All in all, the terms of double tax treaties can be immensely complex, although on a simple level they can provide for one country to have primary taxing rights over certain sources of income and gains. This is often more attractive than being subject to tax in both countries and then claiming a tax credit for the overseas tax paid.

Permanent Establishment

Usually if an individual has business activities in Country X which does not have a tax treaty with his country of residence, Country Y, the domestic tax laws of Country X will apply when deciding where the profits of the business will be taxed. This will usually mean the profits will be fully taxed in Country X.

However, if there is a double tax treaty between Country X (country of residence) and Country Y (country where business activities carried out) business profits are not taxed in Country Y if there is no permanent establishment in Country Y – the profits will only be taxed in Country X where the trader is resident.

By contrast if a permanent establishment does exist in the overseas country, only the income derived from that permanent establishment is taxable.

This is clearly of great benefit to international traders as it could restrict their tax liability in overseas jurisdictions.

What is a Permanent Establishment?

The definition of a permanent establishment varies from treaty to treaty. Generally, the determination of whether a permanent establishment exists depends on two key issues:

- The existence of a fixed place of business
- The presence of dependent agents

If a business has a facility such as a branch, an office, a factory, a construction site and so on, it will usually be deemed to have a permanent establishment. However, even if the business has one of these, it will not be deemed to have a permanent establishment if the facility is used solely for 'preparatory or auxiliary' activities.

If a business has an agent in a treaty country who operates on its behalf and who exercises authority on its behalf to conclude contracts, this would indicate that there is a permanent establishment.

Not all types of agents would be caught within the permanent establishment rules. A notable exception is commission agents who might generate orders but don't have the authority to actually bind the 'principal'.

How to Avoid Overseas Activities Being Classed as a Permanent Establishment

- **Only carry out 'preparatory or auxiliary' activities**. As mentioned above, a business won't have a permanent establishment if its activities in the treaty country amount to just 'preparatory or auxiliary' activities.

  In order to get classed within this category you'd be looking at activities that lead up to future trading – for example, making enquiries or 'testing the water' in overseas markets.

- **Shortening the duration of construction, installation or consultancy projects**. Whether a construction, installation or consultancy project constitutes a permanent establishment usually depends on how long the project lasts. For example, some treaties provide that a permanent establishment includes activities that continue for a period of more than six months. Provided you can ensure your activity in a particular country is less than this, there may be no permanent establishment.

- **Using independent agents to carry out business.** Tax treaties usually provide that using agents will not constitute a permanent establishment. Typical provisions provide that:

  "an enterprise of a Contracting State shall not be deemed to have a permanent establishment in the other Contracting State merely because it carries on business in that other State through a broker, general commission agent or any other agent of an independent status, provided that such a person is acting in the ordinary course of his business."

In view of this, it's worth considering the advantages of using independent agents to carry out business in other countries. (Note that in addition to the potential tax benefits, there are other benefits in using independent agents to carry out business, for example better knowledge of local customers.)

Dividends, Interest and Royalties

As we've already seen, many overseas countries will not only try to tax your business profits but will also levy a withholding tax on dividends paid to shareholders.

As a result, the total foreign taxes payable in an overseas country may be much higher than the income or corporation tax you suffer in your home jurisdiction.

This is where tax treaties come to the rescue. They can help to alleviate this problem by providing reduced rates of withholding tax on dividends.

Usually tax treaties provide relief in the form of lower tax rates for interest income or royalties and this may give rise to tax planning opportunities.

Example

Investco, resident in Country 3, is thinking of investing in Country 1. Investco also has a subsidiary (Subsidco) in Country 2. If the withholding tax rate between Country 1 and 2 is lower than that between Country 1 and the 3, Investco may consider using its subsidiary in Country 2 to carry out the investment, to take advantage of the lower withholding tax rate.

At this point it's worth mentioning 'treaty shopping'. If the arrangement in the above example has no commercial purpose other than avoiding taxes, it might be regarded as 'treaty shopping'.

Treaty shopping involves the use of a tax treaty by a person who is a resident of a third country (in other words not a resident of one of the two countries covered by the tax treaty).

A common example of this is the use of the Netherlands to route royalty income to benefit from the lower rates of withholding tax.

The problem of treaty shopping is worst for countries like the US which has withholding taxes which vary from treaty to treaty. As a result taxpayers have frequently taken advantage of the most favourable treaty.

However, all recent tax treaties entered into by the US include what's known as a limitation on benefits article. The main purpose of this article is to deny treaty benefits to a company that is resident in one of the treaty countries but is in effect serving as a channel for residents of a third country.

If the article applies it will prevent the lower withholding taxes applying. So this could easily scupper any plans for using treaties to obtain lower withholding taxes. Note this problem only arises if there is a limitation of benefits article.

Elimination of Double Taxation

One of the basic objectives of tax treaties is to prevent income being taxed twice. This objective is generally achieved by an 'elimination of double taxation' provision which usually has similar wording to the following clause from the double tax treaty between the UK and Spain:

"Where a resident of Spain derives income which, in accordance with the provisions of this Convention, may be taxed in the United Kingdom, Spain shall allow as a deduction from the tax on the income of that person an amount equal to the tax paid in the United Kingdom – such deduction shall not, however, exceed that part of the tax, as computed before the deduction is given, which is appropriate to the income derived from the United Kingdom. The tax paid in the United Kingdom shall also be allowed as a deduction against the corresponding Spanish prepayment taxes.

In essence this ensures you aren't taxed twice on the same income. In the case of the UK this provision is actually pretty superfluous as the UK operates its own system of double tax relief. This means that even if there is no double tax treaty in existence, a UK resident with overseas income would still usually get double tax relief.

The elimination of withholding taxes makes an effective treaty network a valuable weapon in any tax minimisation 'arsenal'.

This is particularly the case for offshore groups and for international trading, particularly in a group structure. This is where many tax havens fail to deliver as they are unlikely to have any established treaty network. Instead countries such as the UK, Cyprus, Ireland and Gibraltar offer great opportunities.

Overseas Workers

If you're going overseas on a secondment you should also look at the relevant double tax treaty to see if it can yield any tax benefits.

In the case of the UK, overseas workers who come to the UK and spend between six and twelve months in the UK may be able to make use of a suitable double tax treaty with the country they come from.

Certain treaties will allow salary to be exempted from UK tax if a worker's presence in the UK is less than 183 days during the tax year.

However, in order to qualify for this exemption the worker will need to satisfy a couple of conditions:

- Firstly, they must be tax resident in the other country.
- Secondly, the employer must be a non-UK employer who doesn't recharge the UK company for the worker's services and shouldn't claim a UK tax deduction for the UK salary.

Each treaty is different so you'll need to examine the particular treaty between your home country and where you'll be working to see if you qualify. Some treaties prevent tax year straddling by specifying that the presence in the UK must be for less than 183 days.

Avoiding Capital Gains Tax (CGT)

UK residents usually pay CGT on their worldwide capital gains.

Tax planners used to suggest becoming non-resident/not ordinarily resident for one tax year and disposing of assets before returning to the UK.

The UK Government subsequently tightened up the rules and now it is pretty much impossible to escape capital gains tax by leaving the country for a short time.

A UK resident would now normally need to be non UK resident for five complete tax years to avoid paying capital gains tax on profits.

In the period to April 5th following your departure, your gains are taxed in the year the gain arises. From April 6th after your departure to the date of your return, your gains are taxed in the year you return (unless your are not resident for five full tax years or the gain is from assets bought and sold while not resident).

Therefore if you're UK resident, you'll be subject to the five year non residence requirement to avoid UK capital gains tax, irrespective of what any double tax treaty says.

Chapter 11

Other Important Tax Haven Benefits

Deemed Uplift on Immigration

As we've seen tax havens essentially fall into three categories:

- Nil tax havens such as the Bahamas and British Virgin Islands
- Low tax havens such as Malta and Gibraltar
- Countries operating a territorial exemption such as Panama and Costa Rica

However, any discussion of tax havens wouldn't be complete without looking at the full picture and considering some of the other ways that other countries allow you to minimise your tax burden.

Certain high-tax countries also offer rules that could help you slash your tax bill – it's just a case of knowing how to use them. For example, some countries such as:

- Australia
- Canada
- South Africa
- Germany

offer what's known as a deemed uplift in the value of your assets on immigration. This rule can save you thousands in capital gains tax.

Although you may have bought an asset for next to nothing years ago, your cost for tax purposes in your new country of residence is deemed to be the market value at the date of immigration.

In most cases this means that if you sell the asset shortly after obtaining residence you will not realise a gain – the selling price and the 'cost' will be roughly the same (the market value of the asset).

All that will be taxed is any gain that has arisen since the date of immigration.

This type of planning can usually apply to either assets held personally or also assets held within a trust or other entity.

What Happens When You Leave the Country?

The other side of this tax break is that if the immigrant subsequently leaves the country there is then likely to be a deemed disposal of assets at the date of emigration.

Note that in Australia and Germany special elections can be made to avoid this and in Canada individuals who have been resident in Canada for less than 5 years can be exempt from the tax on emigration.

Continuing Liabilities

Just because you cease to be a resident of a particular country does not mean that it will cease to take an interest in you.

In the UK, for example, an expatriate may be liable to capital gains tax on assets held at departure if sold within five UK tax years and you return within that period. Countries such as Spain and Germany will continue to tax certain expatriates for a number of years if they move to a tax haven jurisdiction.

Others such as Iceland will tax the expatriate for a while until they become resident in another jurisdiction – sometimes in these circumstances it may be useful and quite easy to obtain resident status in a favourable tax jurisdiction such as Gibraltar or Malta (by making use of the HNWI or permanent residence schemes).

The European Tax Havens

We've covered a lot of the Caribbean tax havens and whilst many of these offer 0% tax it's important to note that for individuals living in Europe there are lots of opportunities closer to home.

The EU Parent/Subsidiary Directive on dividends can be a useful tool. In particular, an increasing trend is for certain EU countries such as Malta and Cyprus to be used as a channel for interest and royalty income arising outside the EU. Crucially the directive doesn't contain a limitation on benefits clause which makes it much more beneficial for use as channel for funds.

As we've seen Cyprus is a particularly good choice for investments in Eastern Europe given its strong treaty network and many provide for 0% withholding tax on interest, royalties and dividends. This can therefore allow the disposal of property in Eastern Europe and the extraction of proceeds free of taxes.

Cyprus itself offers a highly advantageous capital gains regime with no gain charged on the disposal of shares or land unless the land is located in Cyprus or the shares are in a Cyprus property investment/dealing company.

Malta can also be considered a potential low tax jurisdiction and in terms of lifestyle it's popular due to the low property prices, low crime rate and Mediterranean climate.

Another less well known European tax haven is Estonia. An Estonian company pays no tax on its income and shares can often be sold free of taxes.

Investing in the UK

The UK has become a hot spot for property investment and many non-residents want to know how to invest in the UK whilst minimising their UK tax.

A non-resident should be able to structure his investment so that no income tax, capital gains tax or inheritance tax is payable. A common plan is to use a nil tax trust (for example, in the Channel Islands) to invest through a zero tax company (for example, in the British Virgin Islands) which would lend money to the company. The company would be allowed a deduction for the interest.

You need to be careful about this and only provide debt to the extent a third party would. The Inland Revenue will generally accept a loan of 75-85% of the cost, charged on the property. The interest deduction would in practice significantly reduce or even eliminate the UK taxable profits, particularly if an interest only loan was used. As the property is owned by an offshore IBC there would be no question of UK capital gains tax or inheritance tax being levied.

Certificates of Tax Exemption

Some tax havens, particularly the Caribbean ones, offer what's known as 'certificates of tax exemption'. Essentially these are a promise by the government that no tax will be levied on your income or gains whilst you are a resident (usually for a certain number of years, such as 20 years).

These exemptions give you some certainty in your affairs which is valuable considering the expense of setting up an offshore structure.

Countries such as the Bahamas, British Virgin Islands, St Kitts and Nevis and Panama all offer exemptions.

The Concept of Domicile

Aside from residence, sometimes a country will use the concept of domicile which will have an impact on how residents are subject to tax.

Domicile is a different concept from residence and in many countries it may not even be relevant. In the UK it is relevant for inheritance tax purposes as well for assessing the chargeability of overseas income and gains. It also has implications for estate tax in the USA.

Domicile implies a much stronger relationship with a country than simple residence. The residence test is usually satisfied by spending a certain number of days each tax year in a country.

Domicile usually means that you make a country your permanent home. This is satisfied if you were born in the country or if you live there with the intention of making it your permanent home.

In jurisdictions such as the UK, Ireland and Barbados and Malta, an individual's liability to income tax will be affected by their domicile status.

In these countries there is a clear distinction between a person's domicile and physical residence for tax purposes. In effect, a 'foreign' person resident in, for example, the UK or Ireland will only be taxed on foreign income sent back to the UK or Ireland.

These countries therefore offer excellent opportunities for immigrants to minimise taxes where they have income that is generated offshore.

Some countries such as Japan apply a similar concept to domicile. Japan, for example, generally only taxes non-permanent residents on their Japanese source income and on foreign income that is remitted to Japan.

Individuals will be non permanent residents provided they do not intend to permanently reside in Japan and have resided in Japan for fewer than five years.

Capital and Income Accounts

A common technique to maximise the use of non domicile status is to use separate income and capital accounts.

This allows a distinction to be made between capital and subsequent income from capital (such as interest) before taking up permanent residence and can even allow tax free living in the above countries in certain cases.

It is often advisable for foreign domiciliaries to have at least three overseas bank accounts:

- The first account for existing capital

- The second account to deposit the proceeds of any asset disposals

- The third account to contain the interest from the first two accounts, along with any other foreign source income

The point of this exercise is to segregate your foreign income and gains.

If you want to bring money into the country you should first remit funds from the first account. This can usually be done free of tax.

If further funds are required, then withdrawals can be made from the second account, which could effectively subject the withdrawals to capital gains tax. However, this would depend on your country of residence. Malta for example would not tax these gains and in the UK and Ireland there would be reliefs to reduce any tax payable.

Finally, withdrawals from the third account would be subject to income tax.

Tax Sparing Provisions

We touched on these earlier in the book – they allow a deduction for taxes that have not actually been suffered.

This applies so that if tax is 'spared' or exempted in one country, then it is credited against your tax bill in your home country as if it had actually been paid in the first country.

The purpose of these provisions is usually to encourage foreign investment in developing countries.

These provisions encourage direct foreign investments in the tax sparing country as the foreign investors enjoy a better return on their money because of the potential tax credit they can get from their home authorities.

Example – Malaysia

Malaysian tax treaties often include 'tax sparing' arrangements. A dividend that is distributed out of profits which have been exempted
from tax under the Malaysian tax incentive regime, is deemed to be have been paid out of profits that have been subject to tax.

This is so as to enable a non-resident to claim a tax credit on the exempt dividend in his home country.

This also applies to interest on certain loans and royalties.

Cyprus

Cyprus has some extremely favourable tax sparing provisions which apply to the following countries:

- Canada
- Czech Republic
- Denmark
- Egypt
- Germany
- Greece
- India
- Ireland
- Italy
- Malta
- Poland
- Romania
- United Kingdom

However, these provisions look like they are now on their way out. The OECD has recommended that they be abolished given the potential for abuse.

Need Affordable & Expert Tax Planning Help?

Try Our Unique Question & Answer Service

The purpose of this guide is to provide you with detailed guidance on using tax havens.

Ultimately, you may want to take further action or obtain guidance personal to your circumstances.

Taxcafe.co.uk has a unique online tax service that provides access to highly qualified tax professionals at an affordable rate.

No matter how complex your question, we will provide you with some help through this service. The cost is just £69.95.

To find out more go to **www.taxcafe.co.uk** and click the Tax Questions button.

TAX*Cafe*™

Pay Less Tax!

... with help from Taxcafe's unique tax guides, software

All products available online at **www.taxcafe.co.uk**

➢ **How to Avoid Property Tax** - Essential reading for property investors who want to know all the tips and tricks to follow to pay less tax on their property profits.

➢ **Non Resident & Offshore Tax Planning** - How to exploit non-resident tax status to reduce your tax bill, plus advice on using offshore trusts and companies.

➢ **Using a Property Company to Save Tax** - How to massively increase your profits by using a property company... plus all the traps to avoid.

➢ **How to Avoid Inheritance Tax** - A-Z of inheritance tax planning, with clear explanations and numerous examples. Covers simple and sophisticated tax planning.

➢ **How to Avoid Stamp Duty** - Little known but perfectly legal trade secrets to reduce your stamp duty bill when buying or selling property.

➢ **Grow Rich with a Property ISA** - Find out how to invest in property tax free with an ISA.

➢ **Using a Company to Save Tax** - Everything you need to know about the tax benefits of using a company to run your business.

➢ **Bonus vs Dividend** - Shows how shareholder/directors of companies can save thousands in tax by choosing the optimal mix of bonus and dividend.

> **How to Avoid Tax on Your Stock Market Profits** - How to pay less capital gains tax, income tax and inheritance tax on your stock market investments and dealings.

> **Selling a Sole Trader Business** - A potential minefield with numerous traps to avoid but significant tax-saving opportunities.

> **How to Claim Tax Credits** - Even families with higher incomes can make successful tax credit claims. This guide shows how much you can claim and how to go about it.

> **Property Capital Gains Tax Calculator** - Unique software that performs complex capital gains tax calculations in seconds.

Disclaimer

1. Please note that this tax guide is intended as general guidance only for individual readers and does NOT constitute accountancy, tax, investment or other professional advice. Taxcafe UK Limited and the author accept no responsibility or liability for loss which may arise from reliance on information contained in this tax guide.

2. Please note that tax legislation, the law and practices by government and regulatory authorities (eg Inland Revenue) are constantly changing and the information contained in this tax guide is only correct as at the date of publication. We therefore recommend that for accountancy, tax, investment or other professional advice, you consult a suitably qualified accountant, tax specialist, financial adviser, or other professional adviser. Please also note that your personal circumstances may vary from the general examples given in this tax guide and your professional adviser will be able to give specific advice based on your personal circumstances.

3. Please note that Taxcafe UK Limited has relied wholly upon the expertise of the author in the preparation of the content of this tax guide. The author is not an employee of Taxcafe UK Limited but has been selected by Taxcafe UK Limited using reasonable care and skill to write the content of this tax guide.

Printed in the United Kingdom
by Lightning Source UK Ltd.
126140UK00001B/181-183/A